THREE TYPES OF
RELIGIOUS PHILOSOPHY

Books by Gordon H. Clark

Readings in Ethics (1931)
Selections from Hellenistic Philosophy (1940)
A History of Philosophy (coauthor, 1941)
A Christian Philosophy of Education (1946, 1988)
A Christian View of Men and Things (1952)
What Presbyterians Believe (1956)[1]
Thales to Dewey (1957)
Dewey (1960)
Religion, Reason and Revelation (1961, 1986)
William James (1963)
Karl Barth's Theological Method (1963)
The Philosophy of Science and Belief in God (1964, 1987)
What Do Presbyterians Believe? (1965, 1985)
Peter Speaks Today (1967)[2]
The Philosophy of Gordon H. Clark (1968)
Biblical Predestination (1969)[3]
Historiography: Secular and Religious (1971)
II Peter (1972)[2]
The Johannine Logos (1972)
Three Types of Religious Philosophy (1973, 1989)
First Corinthians (1975)
Colossians (1979, 1989)
Predestination in the Old Testament (1979)[3]
I and II Peter (1980)
Language and Theology (1980)
First John (1980)
God's Hammer: The Bible and Its Critics (1982, 1987)
Behaviorism and Christianity (1982)
Faith and Saving Faith (1983)
In Defense of Theology (1984)
The Pastoral Epistles (1984)
The Biblical Doctrine of Man (1984)
The Trinity (1985)
Logic (1985, 1988)
Ephesians (1985)
Clark Speaks From the Grave (1986)
Logical Criticisms of Textual Criticism (1986)
First and Second Thessalonians (1986)
Predestination (1987)
The Atonement (1987)
The Incarnation (1988)

[1] Revised in 1965 as *What Do Presbyterians Believe?*
[2] Combined in 1980 as *I & II Peter.*
[3] Combined in 1987 as *Predestination.*

THREE TYPES OF RELIGIOUS PHILOSOPHY

by
Gordon H. Clark

The Trinity Foundation
Jefferson, Maryland

Three Types of Religious Philosophy
© 1973 Elizabeth Clark George and
Lois A. Zeller. Second edition
© 1989 The Trinity Foundation
Post Office Box 169
Jefferson, Maryland 21755
Printed in the United States of America
ISBN 0-94093-21-4

Contents

Foreword

Three Types of Religious Philosophy may be a forbidding title to most Americans, including many American Christians, who are not interested in philosophy. Perhaps they think that philosophy is for scholars, those sheltered residents of ivory towers who do not have to deal with the "real world." Perhaps they simply feel overwhelmed by the difficulty of the arguments.

Still worse, they may ask, What has Christianity to do with philosophy? Does not the apostle Paul warn us not to be deceived by philosophy? Surely we have better things to do than read about philosophy, let alone three different types. Why, then, a book by this title?

To reply: Just as all men speak prose whether they know it or not, so all men, not simply philosophers, have a philosophy. There is no possibility of a rational being not having a philosophy. And if all men speak prose, the question is not prose or no prose; the only question is whether they shall speak it correctly or not. Similarly the question is not philosophy or no philosophy; the only question is whether a man's philosophy shall be correct or not.

Second, Paul warns us very strongly, not against all philosophy—that would be even more absurd than urging men not to speak prose—but against unbiblical philosophy: "Beware lest anyone cheat you through philosophy and empty deceit according to the tradition of men, according to the basic principles of the world, and not according to Christ." Paul is warning us, not about all philosophy, but about non-Christian philosophy. *Philosophy* means the love of wisdom. Christ is the

Wisdom of God, according to John and Proverbs, and true philosophy consists in the love of God.

There is, however, much confusion among both ordinary Christians and their leaders about philosophy. Many Christian leaders, in fact, teach philosophies according to the tradition of men, according to the basic principles of the world, and not according to Christ. Examples abound. Let me suggest just one: the belief that the shroud of Turin is the burial cloth of Christ.

Many Protestants share Roman Catholicism's religious philosophy, empiricism, the notion that truth comes through the senses: seeing, hearing, smelling, tasting, touching, and perhaps a few more. (The empiricists have not yet furnished us with a complete list of the senses.) This empiricism, with its emphasis on the importance of experience, has led to a growing acceptance of relics and rituals, which appeal primarily to the senses. There is a great and growing abandonment of the intellectual Word in worship in favor of the empirical smells and bells of Roman, Episcopal, and Orthodox liturgy. Ritual and rote are fast replacing sermons and study in church.

One indication of the growing Protestant affinity for Rome's religious philosophy is the sympathetic reception the Catholic Church's claims about the shroud of Turin have received from certain Protestants.* The chairman of the Department of Philosophy at the Baptist, fundamentalist Liberty University, Gary Habermas, published a book in 1981 (actually a Roman Catholic publisher, Servant Books, published it) arguing that the shroud was, in fact, the burial cloth of Christ. He solemnly declared that "there is no practical possibility that someone other than Jesus was buried in the shroud."

---

* Even while he was announcing the results of the latest scientific tests showing that the shroud could be dated only to the fourteenth century, Cardinal Ballestro of Turin assured his audience that "the holy shroud has produced miracles and continues to."

Nor is Mr. Habermas's statement the only example of philosophical incompetence supporting religious superstition. A leader of the scientific team that investigated the shroud in October 1979, Thomas D'Muhala, a "born-again" Christian, also asserted, "Every one of the scientists I have talked to believes the cloth is authentic. Some say, maybe this is a love letter, a tool he left behind for the analytical mind."

In 1979, after a team of scientists had examined the shroud, a leading conservative lawyer in the "pro-family" movement had this to say about the shroud of Turin:

At long last, we have the proof demanded by the doubting Thomases. The proof is the shroud in which the body of Jesus was wrapped, and is now preserved at Turin, Italy, in the Cathedral of St. John the Baptist.

A recent movie called *In Search of Historic Jesus* shows the Shroud and details its proof. The Shroud bears many scourge marks from the back of the body it wrapped. It shows marks of thick, tightly compressed long hair, gathered at the back of the neck, in the unique fashion of young Jewish men of the first century.

The front of the Shroud shows the wound in the side and the prints of the nails on both wrists—not through the hands, as portrayed on most crucifixes . . .

The thumbs are pulled tightly into the palms of the hands, in accordance with the reflex which medical science tells us would result from the nail wounds in the wrists. The knees appeared severely damaged as if from repeated falls.

Close examination reveals abrasions on the shoulder which could come from carrying the cross. The nose is broken and the beautiful face is disfigured by violence.

The body shown by the Shroud is muscular, and devoid of any excess weight. The body is estimated to have weighed 170 pounds and to have a height of 5 feet 11 inches. The man's age appears to be between 30 and 36 years, and the appearance is majestic.

There are eight independent puncture wounds of the scalp

which could have been caused by the crowning of thorns. . . .

The evidence of the murder of Jesus Christ is far greater than of Julius Caesar's murder by Brutus and others. We have no modern proof of the wounds which killed Caesar. We don't have the shroud in which Caesar was buried.

We cannot match the accounts of Caesar's murder with his shroud, as the accounts in the four Gospels perfectly match the body marks on the Holy Shroud. . . .

The Shroud provides overwhelming proof of the accuracy of the Gospels' history of the crucifixion of Jesus.

Likewise, the Shroud gives proof of the Resurrection. The numerous experts who examined the Shroud within the last year, including all varieties of Christians, Jews, agnostics, and atheists, have concluded that the body suddenly left it with a great burst of radiation-like energy. . . .

The Shroud proves the most remarkable miracle in history.

Now the writer of those words, Phyllis Schlafly, is a well-educated lawyer and quite famous. She is a Roman Catholic who has preached at Thomas Road Baptist Church, Jerry Falwell's church, in Lynchburg, Virginia. She knows—or rather, she ought to know—that the shroud does not and cannot provide "overwhelming proof of the accuracy of the Gospels," and that it certainly does not "give proof of the Resurrection." But she is an empiricist, and thus is blind to the logical gaps in her argument. It is precisely such logical voids between premises and conclusions that characterize superstition.

But we need not restrict our charges of incompetence and superstition to lawyers and philosophy teachers. The infallible popes themselves have expressed their belief in the authenticity of the shroud. Nineteen popes have expressed their confidence in the authenticity of the shroud. Pope Paul VI called the shroud "The most important relic in the history of Christianity." Between 1472 and 1480, Pope Sixtus IV issued four bulls indicating that he believed the shroud to be worthy of the highest veneration. In 1506 Pope Julius II proclaimed the Feast of the Holy Shroud. In 1950, Pius XII addressed the First International Shroud Congress and expressed his wish that the participants at the Congress contribute even more zealously to spreading the knowledge and veneration of so "great and sacred a relic."

What has all this to do with religious philosophy? The case of the shroud of Turin graphically illustrates some of the matters at issue between empiricism, which is the dominant religious philosophy of the twentieth century, and Biblicism, which is the Christian view.

A Biblicist, that is, one who assumes what the Bible says is true as an axiom, a first principle, would have known from the start that the shroud of Turin was a fake. The Bible says quite clearly,

> After this Joseph of Arimathea, being a disciple of Jesus, but secretly, for fear of the Jews, asked Pilate that he might take away the body of Jesus; and Pilate gave him permission. So he came and took the body of Jesus. And Nicodemus, who at first came to Jesus by night, also came bringing a mixture of myrrh and aloes, about a hundred pounds.
> Then they took the body of Jesus, and bound it in strips of linen with the spices, as the custom of the Jews is to bury. . . .
> Then Simon Peter came, following him, and went into the tomb; and he saw the linen cloths lying there, and the handkerchief that had been around his head, not lying with the linen cloths, but folded together in a place by itself.

A Biblicist should not have been fooled by the shroud, and many were not. Christ's body was not covered by one strip of cloth, but wound with several (note the plural *cloths*), together with 100 pounds of spices. Furthermore, his head was wrapped separately from his body.

But an empiricist, one who believes that the evidence of the senses is more certain than the statements in the Bible, one who chooses the authority of the senses rather than the authority of

God, might have been fooled, and many were. Some felt the shroud offered "overwhelming proof" of the death and resurrection of Christ. They have been embarrassed by the latest scientific tests—empirical tests—which seem to show that the shroud dates only to the fourteenth century, not the first. Liberty University's Department chairman, even after the latest scientific findings were made known, asserted that "if the shroud is authentic, it offers incredible [!] further proof of the Crucifixion, and possibly the Resurrection." This statement offers credible further proof that Mr. Habermas simply does not know what proof is.

The case of the shroud of Turin brings into focus the central issue in philosophy: the source of our knowledge. How do we know? Do we trust the authority of our senses (and of science)? Do we trust the authority of the unaided human mind? Or do we trust God? Many professing Christians would agree with Aristotle that knowledge comes through the senses. That is the official position of the Roman church, and the unofficial position of most Protestant churches. Some of those Christians have been avidly promoting the shroud of Turin as empirical evidence of the resurrection of Jesus Christ. It is the evidence that "proves" the Gospels. But the dogmatist must ask: What is proof? Are the Gospels documents the truth of which needs to be proved? Can science and religious relics prove the truth of the Bible? Even more fundamentally, can science or sense experience prove anything at all? *Three Types of Religious Philosophy* answers these questions, and the answers turn the secular philosophical world upside down.

In 1982 *National Review,* the conservative magazine of opinion edited by William F. Buckley, Jr., commented:

> The fact now appears to be that the famous Shroud of Turin has been accurately dated. High-contrast photography reveals a coin placed on the right eye of the figure. The coin can be identified. It depicts a lituus, or astrologer's staff, and the letters

UCAJ can be discerned, part of an inscription referring to Tiberius Caesar. This coin was minted during the procuratorship of Pontius Pilate. Pilate went out of office in 36 A.D., but coin specialists assert that he had coins minted only between 30 and 32 A.D.

Well, that pretty much does it. The Shroud is in fact a kind of photograph of Jesus Christ. The coin pins down the dating.

One intelligent *National Review* reader replied to this asinine argument with these words:

> I have, hermetically preserved between the pages of an old *National Review,* a picture of my Labrador Retriever, revealing a coin placed on the right eye of the dog. The coin can be identified as a zinc penny, minted during the Presidency of Franklin D. Roosevelt. Roosevelt went out of office in 1945, but coin specialists assert that such coins were minted only in 1943.
>
> Well, that pretty much does it. My Labrador was in fact Sergei Rachmaninoff, who died March 28, 1943.

Absurd, you say? But this argument is no more absurd than the arguments purporting to prove that the shroud of Turin is the burial cloth of Christ. In two clever paragraphs the writer exposed a few of the many logical fallacies that the empiricists commit every time they argue. Gordon H. Clark does far more. He demonstrates that empiricism, and rationalism as well, though hardly anyone is a disciple of Anselm these days, is a tissue of logical fallacies.

The result is a classic introduction to religious philosophy that avoids the errors of empiricism and rationalism and presents the Biblical view, which Clark calls dogmatism. One ought to believe the Bible simply because it is the Word of God; there is no greater authority. Empiricism, the belief in the authority of the senses, is a form of philosophy "according to the principles of the world." To try to prove the Bible by relics and science is more absurd than trying to find the sun with a flashlight, and those who do so open themselves not merely to refutation, but to ridicule as well. Those who think themselves wise, as well as humble laymen, would do well to read this book, for until Christians, especially university professors, get their philosophy straight, the superstitions of the twentieth century will continue to grow, and we shall continue our rapid retreat into the Dark Ages.

John W. Robbins
November 18, 1988

I

INTRODUCTION

What is religion? A book on philosophy of religion ought to be able to define religion, for otherwise the readers would not know what the book is talking about. Then, too, someone will ask, what is philosophy? But, however proper and methodical it might be to begin with these definitions, they will be omitted here.* So numerous are the complexities (one book, some years ago, listed about one hundred definitions of religion) that a straightforward exposition would be as tedious as a ponderous tome on mathematics. Instead, let us try a more colloquial approach.

Common opinion believes that religion has something to do with God. Ordinarily also with a future life. Religion ought also concern the present life, its principles of morality, and just possibly it carries implications on questions of civil government.

Consider some more complexities. If religion has to do with God and human life, religion must say something about the world in which we live. Did God create it? The book of Genesis says he did. How does he govern it—if he does? Morality would seem to be meaningless if the world, including man, were subject to inviolable laws of mechanism. But to replace mechanical laws with providence or teleology, religion must dabble in physics. Then too, since we discuss all these

---

* Compare Gordon H. Clark, *Religion, Reason, and Revelation* (Jefferson, Maryland: The Trinity Foundation, 1986 [1961]).

topics by using our minds and by depending on what we have already learned, our processes of learning must be examined. If our methods of learning are faulty, their conclusions will lead us astray in religion as well as in science.

With the mention of all these subjects (ethics, science, politics, epistemology or theory of learning) philosophy seems to have replaced religion. A devout Christian is interested in Biblical doctrines such as the Trinity and the Atonement. He may not be interested in science or epistemology. Religious minds are not necessarily interested in philosophy. Equally unfortunate is the fact that some philosophical minds are not interested in religion.

This would be all the more unfortunate if philosophy and religion turn out to be identical. Many people think that this could not possibly be the case. But are not the two subjects related to each other? Orthodox theologians often defend their theology against scientific attack. They must therefore study science. And if religion is not some compartmentalized side show, if it is the deepest and controlling issue of life, the relationships among all of life's interests fall under the title of religion. So voluminous are all the subjects mentioned, so numerous also their points of contact, so all-inclusive is their importance, that it is quite plausible to identify philosophy and religion. The Roman Catholic scholar, Etienne Gilson, wrote that Calvinism has no philosophy. Of course it has no Aristotelian or Thomistic philosophy; and M. Gilson was speaking out of a long-standing and widely accepted tradition that while philosophy and religion may overlap a little, they are essentially distinct. But if one does not accept Gilson's definitions and the Thomistic system, the possibility that philosophy and religion are identical remains open.* Thomism will be discussed in due time: It will not at this point be assumed true.

---

* *Reason and Religion* (New York: Harcourt, Brace, Jovanovich, 1972), by Rem. B. Edwards, though non-Thomistic, similarly defines revelational philosophy *hors de*

As the opening paragraph hinted, the present method will not begin systematically with the definitions of philosophy and religion. What might be called a catch-as-catch-can procedure will survey the whole field from several angles. Perhaps *catch-as-catch-can* suggests too great a degree of randomness. This is reduced, however, by remembering that most ordinary people connect God, science, and morality with both philosophy and religion. The connection is not utterly random. Most philosophers too include some discussion of God along with their theories of science and morality. No doubt the subjects receive varying degrees of emphasis. In the history of thought some problems seem to interest one type of philosopher and other subjects interest others. For example, Anselm and Hegel were not greatly concerned with the physical sciences. Aristotle, Hume, and Kant were. The reason is that one type of philosophy faces no great difficulty at one point, whereas another does. Conversely what the latter finds easy to explain causes the former to squirm in discomfort. But in any case the connections among the subjects are not haphazard.

At any rate there can be no reasonable objection against opening a discussion of the philosophy of religion with arguments on the existence of God rather than with the missing definitions. However, it is not just God as a topic that engages our interest. What attracts our attention more and more as the discussion develops is the method used. Different philosophers have used different methods. Two thinkers may both believe in God and yet differ sharply on how to justify the belief. Each one may say that the other's argument is fallacious. More exactly, each one may say that the other's general method is fallacious, so that no amount of adjustment in details could make it valid. It is like trying to fill out a magic square. The aim is to fill in, with consecutive numbers from 1 to 289, the squares of a square

---

combat (pp. 3-4), though later when his own ox is gored he protests "a persuasive, unconventional definition of religion" (p. 57; compare pp. 45 and 52).

seventeen squares on a side, so that the sums of every vertical column, every horizontal row, and the two diagonals are equal. This can be done by starting in the middle square of any side and proceeding diagonally (with some rules on what to do when one comes to the end of a row). But if the puzzle-solver begins by deciding to fill in alternate squares, then it makes no difference where he begins or in what directions he goes, or what subsidiary rules he uses. He will always fail because his initial method is wrong; and no adjustments can make it right. Similarly, if one wants to prove the existence of God, one may start off in a certain way and then find that it is a failure. The prospective philosopher then tries to modify his argument to take care of an objection or two. All the time, the trouble may be with his method, so that no amount of modification will produce the desired result. He must abandon his method and try something completely different.

A concrete example of this could be the argument of Thomas Aquinas. In reply to an objection or two some authors want to correct a few details and make the argument valid. But if Thomas' basic empiricism is wrong, then all such amendments are in vain. One must change the epistemological method.

Hence the major divisions of the present study are not such things as Atheism, Theism, or the immortality of the soul. The divisions are based on certain types of methods. The three types included in this book are Dogmatism, Rationalism, and Empiricism. A fourth method also needs explanation, *viz.,* Irrationalism or Existentialism—only, it is neither a method nor a philosophy; though no doubt as a widely held point of view it can be fitted into the more elastic category of religion.

Dogmatism

Dogmatism is and has been a widely held form of religious method. Among the uneducated who hardly use the name at all it is frequently, though often inconsistently, the position on which they operate. Among the educated dogmatism is a term that is widely held in ill-repute. Indeed, in college circles such is the antagonism against revelational or dogmatic religion that many volumes on the philosophy of religion, by their silence, give the impression that no such view even exists. For example, in his introductory chapter, John K. Koth, *Problems of the Philosophy of Religion* (Chandler, 1971), mentions "ideas and organizations that unified us at an earlier time" (p. 1), and without defining faith he refers to "knowledge and faith" (p. 2); he also speaks of "how we can verify claims that are made within religious traditions" (p. 5), plus some other phrases so generalized that none of them can be shown to include an idea of revelation. His paragraph on how philosophy differs from theology (p. 8) could stand unchanged if the Bible had never been written, and a reference to "the Judeo-Christian tradition" (p. 10) with emphasis on radical transformations of tradition is far too vague to direct one's attention to a divinely given message. If it be suggested that the chapter on Augustine gives orthodox Christianity its proper acknowledgments, one may reply that, without capitalizing on the author's overemphasis on Neoplatonism or on his disparagement of Augustine's argument against Pelagius, there is no acknowledgment of revelation at all.

Similarly silent on the revelational or dogmatic view of religion, or perhaps even more insensitive to it, is *Ways of Understanding Religion* by Walter H. Capps (Macmillan, 1972). At most there is Hendrik Kraemer's five page chapter "Christian Revelation as Critique of Religions" (p. 251), the title of which contains more on revelation than the contents. Kraemer declares that Jesus Christ "is *the* Revelation of God." This

Person is known "from the total witness of apostles and evangelists in the New Testament." The difficulty is that Kraemer does not accept everything these witnesses say. Therefore what he accepts and what he rejects, *i.e.,* his belief or theology, is determined, not by revelation, but by his subjective and personal preferences as to what Jesus Christ ought to have been.

It would not be difficult to adduce further examples. Their flaw consists in their claim to present a fairly comprehensive account of religious phenomena, while they omit the most widespread of all western views. Not all college textbooks, however, are thus defective. A few are more honest. One such is *God and Reason* by Ed L. Miller (Macmillan, 1972). Consider the following instructive quotations from pages 11-13:

> There are, however, two different kinds of theology; revealed and philosophical . . . . They do represent, in general, very different approaches to the knowledge of God. One of the distinctive features of the Judeo-Christian tradition is its belief in a divine self-disclosure: God has intervened in human history and spoken to man; he has unveiled himself in a "special revelation." And the knowledge of God drawn from this revelation is an example of revealed theology. Such theology is sometimes called "dogmatic" (in the best sense of the word) or "confessional" theology because it seeks to elucidate the divinely bestowed articles of faith (dogmas) which it takes as its fundamental and non-negotiable datum. Not unlike the mathematician, the dogmatic theologian begins with certain givens: his system is self-contained and is offered, so to speak, as a package deal. . . .
>
> For the moment we might dwell a bit on the concept of special revelation. If it is accepted that God has indeed revealed himself to man through a supernatural self-disclosure, then there are open to us at least two different interpretations of that special revelation. The more traditional of the two often is called "propositional" view of revelation. As the word suggests, this

view holds the divine revelation is contained in the language, statements, or propositions of a text, such as the Bible . . . (God spoke to men who in turn wrote down what he said).

Often associated with the propositional view of revelation is the traditional doctrine of the inspiration of the Scriptures. . . . One view, sometimes called the "dictation" theory, holds that the writers of the Bible were, like typewriters, completely passive or even oblivious to the promptings of the Spirit. . . . This interpretation, or at least one version of it, was emphatically embraced by Pope Leo XIII in his 1893 encyclical *Providentissimus Deus:* . . . .

This recognition and account of dogmatism is on the whole most excellent. At the very least it is an honest acknowledgment that there is and has been such a view held; and this acknowledgment contrasts with the silence of some other authors. The one part of Miller's account that must be emphatically rejected is his statement that the Pope emphatically embraced the view that the writers of Scripture were like typewriters, oblivious of their surroundings and condition. Although the author continues by quoting a paragraph of the papal encyclical, there is nothing in it that indicates such a view at all. The author completely misunderstands the Pope. Similarly it would be difficult to find a single Protestant theologian who held such a view. If there be one, however, the stenographer or typewriter dictation theory has never been the traditional or majority view.

To end this canvass of textbooks and to return to the main subject, secular philosophers sometimes give the impression that they would rather adopt the least promising and most incredible views than appear to be religious dogmatists. Since the term is so pejorative in connotation, it might seem to have been wise to use the title *Fideism.* This term has the advantage of being less familiar. Since many people do not know its meaning, it would not so instantly arouse opposition and would therefore have been granted a fairer hearing. On the other hand

Dogmatism is a pointed term that pricks one's attention.

Does dogmatism deserve its bad reputation? Well, in the very first place, although the terms *philosophy* and *religion* have been left in their colloquial and ambiguous condition, definition must begin somewhere. A serious study must understand the meaning of at least some of its terms. Since, now, three methods are proposed for examination, it is obligatory right here to define the methods. Only after dogmatism has been defined can one answer the question whether or not it deserves its bad reputation.

The term *dogmatism* therefore designates that method of procedure which tries to systematize beliefs concerning God, science, immortality, etc. on the basis of information divinely revealed in the sacred writings. If Scriptures narrate miraculous events, then the dogmatic theory of science cannot be that of inviolable mechanism (unless, as is unlikely, the miraculous events narrated as history can be completely and satisfactorily described in differential equations). Similarly, if the Scriptures assign to civil government the prerogative of capital punishment for heinous crimes, dogmatic politics cannot be pacifistic.

This philosophical method, or, on another definition of philosophy, this anti-philosophical method faces the objection that the dogmatist is thereby forced to deny truths obtained from other sources. Our consciences, or, since contemporary psychology forbids us to have consciences, our religious sensitivities rebel against war and capital punishment. Now, sensitivities are sources of truth that cannot be denied. Therefore the Bible teaches immoral attitudes because it assigns the power of the sword to the civil magistrate. Similarly, laboratory experiments have placed men on the moon. This proves that laws of physics cannot be doubted. Therefore biblically recounted miracles could never have happened.

It may be unsystematically anticipatory to notice that the dogmatist can make either of two replies. He may, in the first place, deny that the practical successes of science justify the laws of physics. Consider: Certain laws of physics imply that men can be placed on the moon; men have been placed on the moon; therefore the physical laws are true. How plausible, and how fallacious! Consider again: If it was raining, Neville Chamberlain carried an umbrella; Chamberlain in fact carried an umbrella; therefore it was raining. Practical successes (like Chamberlain's?) do not prove the truth of physical laws. The argument is a logical fallacy. On the other hand, one might think that the experimental procedures of physics imply mechanical laws. They do not, of course; but even if they did, the experiments would not warrant extrapolation beyond the narrow limits of the experiment. In addition, since science is constantly changing and its laws are always being revised, the dogmatist may well deny that science establishes any law as absolute. There is, however, a second reply the dogmatist can make. The reply may be irritating to many people, not only to professional scholars but also to men of uneducated common sense. Nevertheless it is a possible reply, and if one wants to study the philosophy of religion, one ought not to dismiss without examination a very profound, a thorough-going, a basic or radical position. The dogmatist may reply: Dogmatism does not conflict with truth from other sources because there are no other sources of truth!

Since this runs counter to common opinion, it might be best to discuss dogmatism last. If one of the other two methods of inquiry is satisfactory, it will not be necessary to discuss it at all.

Rationalism

Rationalism as well as dogmatism must be defined. As before, a method must be recognized for what it is in order to discuss it intelligently. Now, if dogmatism and rationalism were formal contradictories, one definition would suffice: Rationalism would be precisely "not-dogmatism." As a matter of fact, some orthodox theologians come close to using the term *rationalism* in this sense. They mean by it any view that denies special divine revelation. But since such views are significantly different in method, they should be separated and discussed separately. Even when the method of rationalism is more strictly defined, its historical examples need some sorting out. Augustine, in spite of his greatness, or perhaps because of his greatness, is somewhat inconsistent. He certainly is not a strict dogmatist, for he does not base all knowledge on revelation; nor is he a strict rationalist, for he accepts both some revelation and some empiricism. Yet the best one can do with this incisive thinker is to class him a bit uncomfortably with the rationalists. Another historical accident is that some fairly consistent rationalists (presumably all men fall into some inconsistencies at some point or other) have no substantive agreement with Christian themes, while others, no less formally consistent, agree completely with Christian dogma. The student must not avoid these historical differences; but at the same time he cannot hope to understand them except with the help of a strict definition.

Rationalism then is the theory that all knowledge, and therefore all religious knowledge, can be deduced from logic alone, *i.e.* logic apart from both revelation and sensory experience. Anselm and Spinoza are the most perfect examples, with whom Hegel should also be mentioned.

The discussion now continues with some of the historical variations. One difficulty is that some theologians allow two sources of knowledge. Some knowledge we obtain by revelation; other knowledge we work out for ourselves like geometry. Augustine even admits some sensory knowledge. Or, there might be, though not under the present sub-head, a theologian who accepts revelation and sensation, but denies that there is any knowledge based on logic alone. In all of these combinations the theologian must face the problem of the relation between the two sets of truths. This problem is most pointed when one considers the possibility that the two sets of truths are in actual conflict. During the Middle Ages there was a theory of twofold truth that allowed a man to believe in theology what he proved false in philosophy. In the present century Emil Brunner proposed the possibility that a man as a believer could be certain that Jesus was crucified, while as an historian the same man could be uncertain that the event ever happened. But even if the two sets of truths do not conflict, there is a technical philosophical difficulty. The question is how to relate, combine, and unify them. This is really to ask whether two methods are permissible. If one conclusion is obtained by one method and is called knowledge, and if another conclusion is obtained by a different method, can the latter be unambiguously called knowledge too? If two propositions are the result of different procedures, can they have anything epistemologically in common? These questions involve the definition of the term *knowledge*. Can this definition be formulated other than the result of a method? Spinoza and Hegel insist on a unitary method.

But Anselm? That Anselm accepted the truth of Biblical revelation is beyond question. He also devised his famous ontological argument for the existence of God in the *Proslogium* and discussed the Atonement in *Cur Deus Homo*. The Preface to the latter states, "Leaving Christ out of view, as if nothing had ever been known of him, it proves by absolute reasons the impossiblity that any man should be saved without him." The death of the God-Man must be proved "reasonable and necessary," so as to convince one "unwilling to believe anything not previously proved by reason." At the end of the work Anselm's pupil acknowledges, "By this solution . . . I see the truth of all that is contained in the Old and New Testaments, for in proving that God became man by necessity, leaving out what was taken from the Bible, *viz.*, the remarks on the persons of the Trinity and on Adam, you convince both Jew and pagan by the mere force of reason." Similarly in the *Monologium* Anselm says, "in order that nothing in Scripture should be urged upon the authority of Scripture itself, but that whatever the conclusion of independent investigation should declare to be true, should, in an unadorned style, with common proofs and with a simple argument, be briefly enforced by the cogency of reason and plainly expounded in the light of truth."

The point here is not whether Anselm's arguments are valid or not. That comes later. Here the emphasis lies on the method, *viz.*, Anselm used the Bible at times and at other times deduced the same truths without appealing to the Bible. Thus he used a method, here called rationalism, that derives its conclusions from logic alone.

It should be verified by a study of the books in their entirety that the phrases "absolute reasons," "reasonable and necessary," and the single word "reason," mean "logic alone." Anselm's arguments not only exclude revelation, "leaving Christ out of view as if nothing had ever been known of him," they also exclude all appeal to sensory experience. In defining rationalism after dogmatism, it is natural to single out the role of revelation. But there is a third philosophical method, empiricism, yet to be described. Simply by way of anticipation it may be said that Anselm was thoroughly anti-empirical.

Yet he was not the purest of rationalists, as Spinoza was, because he allowed Scripture alongside of "reason." Note again that "reason" must be defined. Dogmatism defines it in a widely different way. Within the rationalistic part of Anselm's mind, reason is logic. True, he does not say so. This precision was left for Descartes and Spinoza to express.

Anselm believed that the whole Christian system could be deduced from and by the necessary principles of logic. The quotation above refers to "*all* that is contained in the Old and New Testaments." But still these truths are guaranteed by revelation also. What is the relationship? Of course, if all truths come from logic and none come by revelation, rationalism is the only possibility. Similarly if all truths are revelational and none come from logic alone, dogmatism is the only possibility. These two are the methods in their pure form. But in the history of the subject many men have asserted the existence of both kinds of truths. In this case there are five possibilities. (1) All the truths of revelation are truths of logic, and all the truths of logic are truths of revelation. (2) All the truths of revelation are truths of logic, but some truths of logic are not truths of revelation. Anselm does not say enough for us to decide whether he belongs to class one or class two. (3) Some but not all truths of revelation are truths of logic and some but not all truths of logic are truths of revelation. (4) All the truths of logic are truths of revelation, but some truths of revelation are not truths of logic. (5) There is no overlapping at all.

In these five cases the philosopher or theologian faces the problem of relating the two types of truth. Adverse criticism raises the possibility that they may conflict. To show that they do not conflict, does the exponent of one of these five cases appeal to reason or to revelation? If he appeals to reason, the truths of revelation disappear because they are now defended by reason. If he appeals to revelation, then it is a matter of revelation that the truths of reason are true. This illustrates the difficulty of acknowledging two types of truth.

The accidents and oscillations of history make it difficult to classify the several authors. They did not specify the five possibilities and hence did not always make their own position clear. For example, Augustine probably belongs to the third type. He mentions truths of reason that are not truths of revelation. Still he might fall under type two if he really held that all revelation could be proved by logic alone. But it is not clear that he did so. It is also difficult to name an example of type four. The fifth possibility, where the areas do not overlap at all, could represent the Medieval theory of twofold truth. The theologians who use two methods ordinarily wish to avoid any contradiction between their two sets of truths. But there is this one instance where contradiction is admitted: Some theses true in philosophy are false in theology and some true theological propositions are false in philosophy. However, since all or most of these men were Aristotelians, they were not rationalists as here defined. Occam, also an Aristotelian, kept the two sets of truths distinct, though he did not make them conflict. And Thomas Aquinas before him accepted the overlapping view. Strictly these Aristotelians had no truths based on logic alone; they were not rationalists; they were empiricists; but they had two sets of truths, revelational and, shall we call it, secular. They illustrate the five possibilities with two sets of truths, and point up the difficulty of using two methods.

A Comparison

Now to return to the methods themselves, some little comparison should be made between dogmatism and rationalism before beginning the introductory sketch of the third method. Let it be clear, however, that this chapter does not judge of the value of any of these positions. Its purpose is simply to stake out the area of investigation.

Rationalism, as here defined, is, in this twentieth century, in as much ill repute as Dogmatism. Descartes, Spinoza, and Leibniz, the great seventeenth-century rationalists, are and ought to be read for their helpful stimulation; but no one accepts their first principles. The pedantic Christian Wolff, their faithful disciple, is not even read. Yet in the nineteenth century and down into the first quarter of the twentieth, Hegel exercised tremendous influence. True, he was not Spinoza redivivus; he even had a different view of logic; nevertheless his absolutism and his dialectic can only be classified as rationalism.

In view of centuries of acceptance, rationalism cannot today be forgotten, even if it is discarded. It has left too deep a mark on contemporary thought. Furthermore, the twentieth century is nearly at an end. Who can say that rationalism will not revive in some form or other? At any rate, it must be understood. Dogmatists too, in spite of their unpopularity, have existed, exist today, and will probably continue. It too should be understood and not ignored as some textbooks do. Therefore a comparison of dogmatism with rationalism proves helpful.

These two methods seem so completely antithetical that an untutored reader might be inclined to conclude that if one of them was religious, the other must have to be irreligious. One method would have to be so obviously irreligious that no one in all history would ever have chosen it as a basis for any religion. On the contrary, one author opened his book by saying, "Dogmatism and rationalism are the two extremes between which religious philosophy perpetually oscillates."* Yet they possess at least one thing in common. Nor is it a trivial similarity.

In the Medieval books, in modern studies, and in the preceding pages an antithesis has been noted between philosophy and theology, truths of logic and truths of revelation, or reason and faith. The last of these three phrases is very common. Thus the impression is made that revelation is antithetical to reason and that theology must be illogical. This is unfortunate. The term "reason" is used differently by different authors. By reason, Spinoza meant logic; but Thomas Aquinas and Hume meant sensory experience.

Now, dogmatism and rationalism are one in their respect for and detailed use of logic. Dogmatism, even more than rationalism, is accused of hair-splitting and logic-chopping. Hence it is misleading to say that one uses reason and is

---

* H.L. Mansel, *The Limits of Religious Thought.* Mansel is not clear-cut in his definitions. He uses the term *rationalism* in its wider theological sense inclusive of empiricism, and his remarks on dogmatism accordingly continue, "Scripture is to the theological Dogmatist what Experience is to the philosophical. . . . It contains in an unsystematic form the positive doctrines which further inquiry has to exhibit as supported by reasonable grounds and connected into a scientific whole." The phrase "reasonable grounds" is unclear.

rational, while the other makes no use of reason and is irrational. Both use reason equally. It is therefore improper to contrast reason and faith. The difference between the two methods is not their detailed use of logic by which they deduce conclusions from premises. Their difference centers in the source of their premises. The dogmatist takes his premises from Scripture and deduces conclusions. The rationalist begins in another way.

Descartes' first acknowledged premise, from which he thought he could deduce God and the world, was the proposition, "I think." But Descartes had a reason for accepting "I think" as true. The reason was that its denial is self-contradictory. Suppose, says Descartes, that there is an omnipotent demon, whose great delight it is to deceive us. He even makes us think that two and two are four, when they are really five. But though the demon can deceive us in mathematics, and all the more in physics, there is one point on which it is impossible for him to deceive us. In order for us to be deceived, we must think. No matter how false the proposition is that we think, it cannot be false that we think. If we did not think, we would not be deceived. Therefore "I think" is a self-authenticating proposition. That is to say, its denial is self-contradictory. If I deny that I think, I must be thinking. Therefore the assertion or proposition, I think, must be true.

Spinoza does it another way. He formulates definitions of substance, attribute, God, and some others, then he posits seven axioms (e.g., That which cannot be conceived through anything else must be conceived through itself; and, If a thing can be conceived as non-existent, its essence does not involve existence), from which, after the fashion of geometry, he infers that God exists. This actual existence in the conclusion presumably justifies the truth of the definitions and axiom. Whatever validly implies existence, it may be said, must be true. Yet, on the other hand, this justification of axioms seems to be the fallacy of asserting the consequent: If Alexander was killed at the battle of

Thebes, Alexander died young; Alexander died young, therefore he was killed in the battle of Thebes. Spinoza then must somehow refute this charge of invalidity. Otherwise his assumptions do not depend on logic alone. Rationalism therefore faces some embarrassment with respect to its first premises. Dogmatism applies logic to premises given in revelation.

If there is both a similarity and a difference in method, there is also a similarity and a difference in substance. The similarity may be logically necessitated; the difference exists more in the accidents of practice and history. First, the similarity.

Dogmatism, accepting the unsystematic teachings of Scripture, not only puts them in systematic form, but also attempts to draw out further implications. For example the Scriptures do not discuss realism, conceptualism, and nominalism by name. But most dogmatists implicitly favor realism as against conceptualism and nominalism. This seems to be required by the Scriptural data. Rationalism is more explicitly realistic. Nominalism is empirical. Extreme nominalism holds that sensory individuals are the only realities. Concepts are sounds in the air, and Platonic ideas are illusions. But dogmatism must use concepts, such as Atonement, Justification, and so on. It cannot restrict the real and knowable universe to sensory individuals. Here rationalism is in full agreement.

Since this similarity is their common difference as against empiricism, the issue can be made clearer by reporting an imaginary dialogue between an empiricist and his rationalistic opponent.

R.   So you say that the universe is composed of individuals?

E.   Yes. All realities are individuals, and general notions are entirely artificial.

R.   A single thing therefore is real, a single tree, for example, a marble, a baseball bat, and an oyster.

E.   Quite so. The world is so full of a number of things, I am sure we should all be as happy as kings.

R.   But concepts of flora, toys, and crustacea are unreal. They do not exist.

E.   Exactly. The Platonic Ideas are totally illusory. There is no need to invent a second world beyond the one we see with our eyes and handle with our hands. One should not multiply entities beyond necessity.

R.   No doubt you see all that very clearly. But I have difficulty thinking it.

E.   Then you should revise your thoughts to conform with your sensations.

R.   Well, in that case, you must help me, for what you say seems to me to contradict what you mean.

E.   I do not see how that can be. I have said precisely what I mean. Nothing exists except individual things.

R.   If so, how can you talk about thoughts and sensations, or trees and marbles?

E.   How can I talk about them! Why, they are sensory individuals. They are the only realities there are to talk about.

R.   But you did not mention the individual reality, namely this particular tree on the lawn. Nor did you mention this single sensation of green. You had collected many sensations into the general notion of sensation, and many trees into a genus tree.

E.   What is wrong with that? Many times it is convenient to talk about a plurality of trees. This discussion itself concerns many and all trees, not just one.

R.   So it does. But your theory concerns just one tree at a time. How would you speak of this tree?

E.   I would just call it a tree. The one over there on the neighbor's lawn is another tree.

R.   But the word *tree* applies equally to both and therefore cannot designate just one individual. To speak of an individual it would be necessary to use a name, a proper noun, as the grammarians call it.

E.   I fail to see much relevance in your remarks. Call the tree Tom or Horace, as you wish.

R.   But how could you carry on a conversation with only proper nouns? Take any page of any book, replace the common nouns with proper nouns, and the text would become meaningless. Besides even names are not individual enough, for Tom can designate that cat as well as this tree; Horace could designate a pet turtle; and both of these are names of many people. Would you now prefer to give individual things numbers from one to infinity? Then replace each common noun on the page with a different number. Nobody could understand it.

E.   I agree that it would be an unusual language. People would have to learn it. Then they would understand. In fact, a notable development in modern philosophy is the construction of a so-called artificial or mathematical language. It will remove the ambiguities of ordinary English and make everything perfectly clear.

R.   The Chinese have a hard time memorizing twenty thousand different characters, while we use only twenty-six letters. I doubt that we could remember the different numbers attached to each tree in Colorado, plus the number of each grain of sand in the Arizona deserts, plus the license numbers on tourist cars.

E.   You talk nonsense.

R.   No, my friend. It is you who advocate nonsense. For even if a man could memorize the number of each individual, he still could not think of the genus tree, or sand, or car.

E.   Why couldn't he? All he would have to do would be to mention one number after another.

R.   Not at all, my good friend. Before he could mention the numbers of three grains of sand, he would have to recognize that that number ($7^{24}+3$) was a grain of sand like number ($17^{56}-1$).

E.   What is so difficult about that? It is simply numbering grains of sand.

R.   But how can the empiricist be sure that the second numbered thing is a grain of Arizona sand and not a Colorado tree?

E.   Now, indeed, you talk nonsense. Who can possibly confuse a grain of sand with a tree?

R.   I think you could and would. The reason, I hope, will be clear. Of course the reason is not an individual sense object, and you may say that it is not real and does not exist. But then, your theory is not real, either. However, before you number the sands of the Sonoran desert, you must recognize that they are all grains of sand. Each one has the same characteristics as every other. If every one of these objects had a totally different set of characteristics, they would not be similar in the least. To number grains of sand you must operate on the basis of similarity. But an X that exists in $(17^{56}-1)$ places at once is not an individual sensory object. Call it a Platonic Idea, if you wish. However you number it, you must use it in order to separate trees from sand before you can number similar things. If you do not number similar things, but only number things, then the sole characteristic of a thing is its number. And in this case you cannot tell whether $(17^{56}-1)$ is a tree or a grain of sand. Even your phrase "individual sensory object" is not an individual sensory object. It is an alleged similarity. And if similarity and individuality are not real, there would be no individuals and you could not explain your theory.

E.   I think you have played some trick on me. When we have completed our linguistic analysis and produced our mathematical language, I shall point out your error.

This dialogue illustrates a similarity between rationalism and dogmatism in philosophic content. They both need what are often called Platonic Ideas or abstract concepts. Between the two methods, however, there is also a difference in philosophic content, more the result of historical accident than of logical necessity. Unlike Anselm, modern rationalists do not believe that the contents of Scripture can be proved true by logic alone. Its statements, not being accepted on divine authority, are sometimes adjudged false. For example, the liberal theologians of the nineteenth century asserted that the Hittite nation never existed and that therefore the Bible makes false historical statements. In the twentieth century some critics take the Scriptures mythologically or existentially and assert that there never was an Adam, but that he is a picture of each of us as we fall into sin and exemplify the Genesis fable. Spinoza had a more plausible explanation. What the ancient authors wrote, he says, depended on the cultural conditions of Biblical times. They described what they saw, but their descriptions, in a sense even their seeing, conformed to the unquestioned opinions of their era. Thus Joshua's long day and the shadow on the dial going backwards* are descriptions of actual events. The events really happened; but the authors "conceived of and related the occurrence as something quite different from what really happened."†

This may be better than the ludicrous attempts of some later German theologians who explained the miracle of the feeding of the five thousand by imagining that a boy took out his lunch and the four thousand nine hundred and ninety-nine followed his example, or that Adam ruined his digestive system with some poisonous fruit and gave his descendents impaired stomachs. In both cases, however, the alleged event is considerably different from the Scriptural statement.

One should not unthinkingly suppose that logic necessitates a denial of miracles. As far as strict rationalism is concerned, Spinoza could have done better by the Biblical texts, even though he would have had to alter in very important respects some of his secondary principles. Since he bases the

---

* Spinoza refers this to Ahaz. It was Hezekiah. Compare II Kings 20:8 ff.

† *Theologico-Political Treatise*, chapter VI; compare chapter II. Elwes, translator, 1895, pp. 93-94.

uniformity of nature on the immutability of the divine mind,* any Biblical miracle, occurring as described, could be regarded as an element in God's eternal plan. Miracles could depend on "the necessity and perfection of the divine nature," as Spinoza requires, and nothing would be true "save only by divine decree." Nor would Spinoza's objection hold that special events imply an imperfection in God's original plan or in his execution of it. The miracle itself, as well as any ordinary historical event, is decreed from eternity and is not a later correction.

Although this would not abrogate rationalism as an epistemological method, such laws of nature and such a God would not be Spinoza's laws and God. If miracles occur according to a necessary divine plan, the laws of nature must be teleological. God must act for a purpose, and these events would be means in accomplishing the divine aim. But Spinoza denied that nature or God is teleological. Descartes before him considered the failure of Medieval physics to be the result of the telelogical method initiated by Plato and Aristotle. God may have purposes, said Descartes, but, since we cannot appeal to revelation, we can never know them. At the same time the tremendous successes Galileo had obtained through the use of mathematics proved the necessity of mechanism. Spinoza agreed; but to be more consistent he identified God and nature and discarded an unknowable teleology as both useless and groundless. *Deus sive Natura* has no purposes, and the processes of spatial phenomena are strictly mechanical.

Mechanism plausibly rules out miracles. It is unlikely, though theoretically possible, that Joshua's long day and Hezekiah's receding shadow can be described in differential equations. It is less likely that such events and the common course of nature can both be described by the same equations.

---

* "I will show that nature cannot be contravened, but that she preserves a fixed and immutable order. . . . As nothing is necessarily true save only by divine decree, it is plain that the universal laws of nature are decrees of God following from the necessity and perfection of the divine nature" (*op. cit.,* pp. 82-83).

Mechanism therefore replaced teleology.

Yet this is not a necessary implication of rationalism. When Spinoza rejected Descartes' proof of his own existence in *Cogito ergo sum,* he justified his definitions and axioms on the ground that they prove the existence of the object defined. This object was God or Nature. But none of these axioms implies that nature is mechanical. The law of the equal angles of incidence and reflection (which can be taken as an example for any law of physics), instead of being deduced from the axioms that prove God's existence, so as to be essential to rationalism, is itself a later axiom assumed in Part II of the *Ethica,* after Proposition XIII. Since it is independent of the original axioms, the laws of physics are not deduced by logic alone from the being of God. Hence the rejection of this or that Scriptural proposition is not a logical necessity for rationalism. Anselm may have been right.

If, however, there is any logical necessity that distinguishes the extent of rationalistic from dogmatic truths, it would seem to lie in the impossibility of deducing historical particularities from universal premises. Logic also cannot demonstrate that there was a Moses, a David, or a Napoleon. In the nineteenth century this complaint was vociferously urged against the non-spinozistic rationalism of Hegel; and Lévy-Bruhl criticizes the earlier Cartesians as not merely distrusting history, but as having an actual antipathy toward it. For Christianity history is indispensable.

Empiricism

If rationalism can produce no history, no physics, and possibly no religion either, most people would pin their hopes on finding another method. This third method is empiricism. In antiquity Democritus and Aristotle, despite important differences, were empiricists. So too Thomas Aquinas in the thirteenth century and David Hume in the eighteenth. The majority of philosophers today are also empirical.

The strict form of empiricism bases all knowledge on sensation alone. The term *experience* is too vague. No doubt a mystic trance is a type of experience, but mystics do not always claim that their trances give knowledge. Plotinus and Dionysius the Areopagite explicitly denied that knowledge was so obtained. Then too an aesthetic response is also an experience, but no philosopher ever tried to deduce all knowledge from an aesthetic response.* Some authors, in the interest of religion, assert a religious experience *sui generis*. Now, aside from the difficulty of finding a basic similarity in the religious experiences of all men, if they do indeed give any knowledge, it is not clear how to integrate it into one system with physics and history. Sensation, however, is more definite and identifiable. Presumably the data of sensation are the same for all people as trances, aesthetic responses, and religious emotions are not. Therefore strict empiricism is the epistemological theory that all knowledge is based on sensation alone.

Of course there are combinations and variations. Kant combined logic and sensation. He based his religion on moral principles, which, as apriori, seem to have no sensory content. He located the moral self in a noumenal world above the world of space and time. Thus adverse criticism can claim that Kant's religion and ethics are empty rationalism. American humanists, having drawn the logical implication of modernism, retain a semblance of religion in their value judgments. These are admittedly developments from sensation, from highly complicated sensory experience no doubt, but from sensation nonethe-

---

* Physicists do indeed choose between two fundamental hypotheses by their aesthetic appeal. Compare Gordon H. Clark, *The Philosophy of Science and Belief in God* (Jefferson, Maryland: The Trinity Foundation, 1987 [1964]), pp. 85, 107-108. But whereas the logic of rationalism is the same for all rational minds, artistic minds do not all react in an identical manner. Thus one physicist enjoys one fundamental equation, while another prefers a different one. Furthermore, these physicists do not try to deduce history or ethics from their axioms.

less. Logical Positivism or Logical Empiricism is empirical *à outrance*. There is no religion, and ethics is meaningless; but the data of perception are accepted with dogmatic fervor. The defense of empiricism in all forms depends on the fact that religious experience, aesthetic response, and mystic trances are not amenable to the public verification that modern thought so insistently demands. Only sensation provides verification. All empirical philosophers, not only Thomas Aquinas but even Kant so far as the content of knowledge is concerned, make their basic appeal to sensation.

The best known application of empiricism to religion is Thomas Aquinas' famous proof of the existence of God. The so-called Cosmological Argument begins with the sentence, "It is certain and evident to our senses that in the world some things are in motion."

To evaluate the argument, one must examine every step made to see whether the whole is logical or whether it contains an invalid syllogism somewhere. One fallacious link would break the chain and render the whole a failure. But there is something more important. Empiricism holds that nothing can be more certain than what appears to our senses. Thus an assertion that a body is moving is the most certain statement that anybody ever made. Of course, this is precisely the reason Thomas began with it. But now, really, is it more certain that a body I see moves than that I think? Philosophies must be evaluated on the ground of what they begin with. The starting point determines all that follows. It is quite clear how to test the validity of a syllogism, but how may one test the original premise? Should we begin by assuming the authority of sensation, the authority of logic, or the authority of God? The problem is how to start. What method shall we choose? Shall our method be dogmatism, rationalism, or empiricism? It is these methods that we must examine.

II

RATIONALISM

Since contemporary philosophers would rather submit to any indignity rather than become dogmatists, the discussion of this frightful possibility can be postponed to the end. Rationalism, though far from popular since the demise of Hegel's absolutism early this century, still provides great and helpful stimulation. No one who wishes to understand the course of thought, the history of ideas, and the sources of present attitudes can possibly ignore it; and one of its greatest exponents was Augustine.

Augustine

Augustine was not a pure rationalist as the term has been defined here, and combinations of any two methods raise the suspicion of inconsistency or unresolved problems; nevertheless even inconsistencies can be instructive. At the very least one will better understand the problem that forced such a great mind to accept knowingly, or fall unknowingly into, suspicious positions.

The problem, the immediate problem for Augustine, was not the truth of some particular theological doctrine. Being a Christian, of course he wanted to defend and propagate the doctrines of the Trinity, the Atonement, and so on. Such doctrines as these make his work a philosophy of religion rather than a secular philosophy. But if one can know that the doctrine of the Trinity is true, one can know something; if, however, one can know nothing, then one cannot know the Trinity; therefore

Augustine has to begin by showing that knowledge is possible.

In the centuries immediately preceding, the first century before Christ and the first three centuries of our era, Greek philosophy was strongly skeptical. To be sure, Plato in the fourth century had met the skeptical sophists of the late fifth century and had defeated them. But after he and his illustrious pupil Aristotle had founded their schools and bequeathed them to successors, Pyrrho about 300 B.C. initiated a school of skepticism that grew in power and influence for at least four hundred years. Even Plato's Academy became skeptical; the Stoics survived but declined in influence after 200 B.C. The Neoplatonist, Plotinus, who died in A.D. 270, severely damaged both Stoicism and skepticism; but even in A.D. 400 Augustine, who personally had passed through a skeptical stage and then had become a Neoplatonic before being converted to Christianity, thought it still necessary to combat the skeptics.

Historically and personally necessary or not, it is logically necessary to show that and how knowledge is possible before concluding that a particular religious doctrine (or, for that matter, a particular law of physics) can be known as true.

The skeptics had collected an arsenal of arguments against the possibility of knowing anything. These arguments have been repeated time and time again. Descartes actually went the skeptics one better. He referred to an omnipotent demon who constantly deceives us. To most people this sounds like such a ridiculous supposition that they tend to ignore it. If at the start we know nothing at all, if we do not even know that something can be known, it follows that we do not know whether a demon is ridiculous or not. A proposition can be judged ridiculous only if it contradicts some exceptionally well-established truth. If nothing has as yet been established, Descartes' demon cannot be known to be ridiculous. Now, rationalists have always met this difficulty squarely. The same cannot be said of the empiricists.

Other objections to the possibility of knowledge are not so radical, nevertheless they should be met. In fact, since other objections do not seem so preposterous, they should all the more be met.

Here are some examples. How and what we see, depends on our eyesight. But some men have "better" eyesight than others: Some men are color blind—in several degrees, and others see so many colors, avant garde artists, that the rest of us accuse them of having hallucinations. Moreover the eyes of the various animals differ from men's. Whose sensations then can be trusted? This skeptical argument was proposed by the ancients. Modern scientists dress it up in more professional language. Light rays when they hit an object and are reflected to our eyes change their wave lengths. Under varying circumstances the amount of change varies. How then can we know which wave length gives us an accurate impression of the visible object?

This much of the skeptical argument against sense experience suffices for the moment. The point to be hammered home is the necessity of showing that knowledge is possible. A Christian hopes to defend the Trinity, the Ten Commandments, and some historical statements. But where can he begin? Is there anything so sure and certain that the distortions of sense and even Descartes' demon cannot overthrow it? What truth is there that is absolutely basic? Is any proposition self-authenticating? Augustine said, Yes.

What Descartes' first truth was has already been explained: I must think, even to be deceived. Augustine did not put it just this way; but though Descartes proudly boasted that he laid the foundations of philosophy on a completely new and original foundation, the strong influence of Augustine lies on his pages for everyone to see.

In fact, Augustine is clearer and more explicit than Descartes. Descartes' first truth is not really "I think," as he said. His first truth is really the laws of logic. "I think" must be true because a person who denies it exemplifies it in his denial and so has contradicted himself. "I think" depends on the laws of logic.

Augustine starts explicitly with logic. You may not know, he says in effect, whether you are awake or asleep; but you cannot help knowing that you are *either* one *or* the other. That is to say, the principle of complete disjunction cannot be doubted. The law of implication is also indubitable: if there are only four elements (earth, air, fire, and water), there cannot be five. And he might have said, All men are mortal, Socrates is a man, therefore Socrates is mortal.

Here is rationalism's strongest position. Neither dogmatism nor empiricism can assail it, though how empiricism can arrive at logic by sensation is something later to be discussed. Consider: Suppose a student who majors in football takes a course in logic; when the instructor repeats the ancient syllogism, the student, whose IQ is not half his weight, replies, I agree that Socrates is a man and that all men are mortal, but please explain to me what in the world that has to do with Socrates' being mortal!

Unfortunately the instructor cannot explain it: He cannot appeal to anything more basic than the laws of logic. But is it unfortunate? Certainly not unfortunate for rationalism. There is nothing more basic on which the axioms of logic depend. All explanation must use them. If an instructor explains a principle of economics, or of chemistry, or what-not, he says, *Because:* Such and such is true *because*—and then the instructor gives a *reason,* from which the thing to be explained can be deduced, or inferred. Therefore logic cannot be "explained" or "proved" or deduced from anything else because it is absolutely and without exception basic.

Augustine goes further and cites examples from mathematics: two plus two, not only are four, but *must* be four. This is no accidental, empirical datum. It is a logical necessity.

Some modern mathematicians disparage this example.

They argue that mathematics is formal; and if two and four are defined in the usual way, it is merely disguised tautology to say that two and two must be four. However, even if the formal theory of mathematics be granted, this objection does not invalidate the validity of the logic involved. Tautologies, too, must obey the laws of inference.

Descartes was not completely original even in his "I think." Augustine had already insisted that it is certainly true that I exist. The skeptic must exist in order to doubt his own existence. Augustine will ask him, Do you know you exist? And what can the skeptic answer?

Augustine pushes still further. He held that the norms of morality were also known and certain. Did not the skeptics themselves claim to be philosophers, *i.e.,* lovers of wisdom? Everyone desires happiness and the philosopher by his actions shows that happiness resides in the truth. The *skeptic,* etymologically, is a seeker of truth. Therefore a denial of the possibility of truth contradicts the spring of all human action.

This moral aspect is one Augustine emphasized. The skeptic eats his dinner as if he knew there were a dinner to eat, and also as if it were good for him to do so. He avoids beating himself over the head with a hammer, as if it were bad for him. When questioned, the skeptic replies, I do not know these things, but they are more probable than other things. Then Augustine zeroes in: A proposition can be probable and known to be probable, only if it resembles or approximates the truth. A person who does not know what is true cannot know what approximates it. A theory of probability must itself be based on the truth. Therefore the skeptic is refuted by the moral quality of his own actions.

If now a modern student thinks that the principles of morality are not so certain as the principles of logic, and that therefore it is doubtful whether or not I ought to seek my own happiness and eat dinner, at least the laws of logic are indubitable. In any case norms, logical or moral, or even aesthetic, if there be such, are necessary and universal truths. They are true not only here and now, but everywhere and all the time. They are not only true for me, but for everybody. Yet I am a limited, finite being with a circumscribed experience. I have never been able to ask Socrates or, farther back, Abraham, whether he used the logical principles I use. Could it be that logic was not logical before Aristotle enumerated all the possible syllogisms?

It seems therefore that finite as I am, I have in my mind something that is eternal. Logic never began and will never end. Mathematics and morality likewise. Such eternal and immutable truths cannot be abstracted from any mutable matrix. They are not the products of the subjective reason of any individual man. There must therefore be an eternal and immutable reason in which these truths have their origin. Either the truths themselves are God and God is truth; or if there be something superior to truth, then this higher being is God. In either case it is proved that God exists.

It would be most interesting to pursue Augustine's philosophy further. After all, only Thomas Aquinas can challenge Augustine's status as the greatest and most brilliant of all Christian philosophers. The student should therefore learn how Augustine relates reason to faith, what the role of sensation is, whether it is possible to know bodies, how one person can communicate with another, and who can teach whom what? Parenthetically one may note that Augustine discussed at length the problems arising from the barbarian invasions and the sack of Rome in A.D. 410. And of course, there is what he considered most important of all—theology. But though most of this must be omitted here, the existence of God is one of the great themes in the philosophy of religion, and on this subject one or two things still remain to be said.

Anselm

Anselm (1033-1109), Archbishop of Canterbury, previously alluded to, tried to improve on Augustine. This is not dishonorable, nor disrespectful. Anselm deliberately adopted Augustine's motto, *credo ut intelligam:* I believe in order to understand. The doctrines of Christianity are revealed in Scripture and accepted as true by faith. Faith saves. If salvation depended on an understanding of philosophy, few would ever get to heaven. Nevertheless, understanding is a laudable aim, and one increases in Christian virtue by increasing his understanding. But unless God first gives the revelation and man first believes it, there would be nothing to understand. Therefore I believe in order to understand.

One thing, among others, that Anselm wanted to understand better than Augustine did, was the existence of God. To this end he wrote out in his *Monologium* a traditional argument based on the Platonic method of hypostatizing goodness, justice, and other eternal ideas. But he was not satisfied. He wanted something clearer and more simple. By a stroke of genius—not any the less so because of its Augustinian inspiration—he hit upon the Ontological Argument. Here it is in full.

And so, Lord, do thou, who dost give understanding to faith, give me, so far as thou knowest it to be profitable, to understand that thou art as we believe, and that thou art that which we believe. And, indeed, we believe that thou art a being than which nothing greater can be conceived. Or is there no such nature, since the fool hath said in his heart, there is no God? (Ps. 14:1). But at any rate this very fool, when he hears of this being of which I speak—a being than which nothing greater can be conceived—understands what he hears, and what he understands is in his understanding; although he does not understand it to exist.

For it is one thing for an object to be in the understanding, and another to understand that the object exists. When a painter first conceives of what he will afterward perform, he has it in his understanding, but he does not yet understand it to be, because he has not yet performed it. But after he has made the painting, he both has it in his understanding, and he understands that it exists, because he has made it.

Hence, even the fool is convinced that something exists in the understanding, at least, than which nothing greater can be conceived. For when he hears of this, he understands it. And whatever is understood, exists in the understanding. And assuredly that than which nothing greater can be conceived cannot exist in the understanding alone. For suppose it exists in the understanding alone: then it can be conceived to exist in reality, which is greater.

Therefore, if that than which nothing greater can be conceived exists in the understanding alone, the very being than which nothing greater can be conceived is one than which a greater can be conceived. But obviously this is impossible. Hence, there is no doubt that there exists a being than which nothing greater can be conceived, and it exists both in the understanding and in reality.

And it assuredly exists so truly that it cannot be conceived not to exist. For it is possible to conceive of a being which cannot be conceived not to exist; and this is greater than one which can be conceived not to exist. Hence, if that than which nothing greater can be conceived, can be conceived not to exist, it is not that than which nothing greater can be conceived. But this is an irreconcilable contradiction. There is, then, so truly a being than which nothing greater can be conceived to exist, that it cannot even be conceived not to exist; and this being thou art, O Lord, our God.

So truly, therefore, dost thou exist, O Lord, my God, that thou canst not be conceived not to exist; and rightly. For if a mind could conceive of a being better than thee, the creature would rise above the Creator: and this is most absurd. And indeed whatever else there is, except thee alone, can be conceived not to exist. To thee alone, therefore, it belongs to exist more truly than all other beings, and hence in a higher degree than all others. For whatever else exists does not exist so truly, and hence in a less degree it belongs to it to exist. Why, then, has the fool said in his heart, there is no God, since it is so evident, to a rational mind, that thou dost exist in the highest degree of all? Why? except that he is dull and a fool!*

Descartes reduced this argument to a syllogism: God, by definition, is the being who possesses all perfections; existence is a perfection; therefore God exists. Spinoza, as was said before, enlarged this into eleven propositions deduced from a set of axioms and definitions.†

A monk, Gaunilo, Anselm's contemporary, attacked his ontological argument. More recently Kant supposedly demolished it. Maybe Hegel reinstated something like it. But now Hegel is dead. The first thing, then, is to consider Kant's critique. It is very intricate and needs close attention.

Kant's Critique

On an earlier page Kant had defined an *idea* as "a necessary conception of reason to which no corresponding object can be discovered in the world of sense" (p. B. 383). When he comes to *The Impossibility of an Ontological Proof* (p. B. 629) he begins, "The conception of an absolutely necessary

---

* As might be expected and even more so, the literature on the ontological argument seems endless. Alexandre Koyré, *L'Idee de Dieu dans la philosophie de St. Anselm,* makes a thorough examination of the historical antecedents of the argument. John H. Hick and Arthur C. McGill, *The Many-faced Argument,* collect essays written from radically different view-points, all contemporary. It also contains fourteen pages of bibliography.

† Karl Barth, *Anselm: Fides Quarens Intellectum,* denies that Anselm's argument is the one used by Descartes and Leibniz, and criticized by Kant. Nobody much agrees with Barth on this point. His arguments, however, are instructive for their own sakes. They could even be said (if one takes the right attitude) to improve on Anselm. But if Barth's interpretation is an "improvement," it is not Anselm's argument.

being is a mere idea, the objective reality of which is far from being established by the mere fact that it is a need of reason."

That an idea has no corresponding object in the world of sense is not inimical to the existence of God, for God is not a sensory object. But this, as Kant intended, highlights the problem of how to prove the objective reality of a non-sensuous object. For Kant, sensation was enough to prove the existence of a chair or a rock; but what does the same for God? Had Anselm used Kantian terminology, he might have affirmed that a necessary concept of reason, since necessary, must have an object. But maybe he would not have so affirmed. The laws of logic are necessities of reason, but they are rules for the conducting of argumentation. They are not external objects. The idea of God as well might then be a necessary concept without having a corresponding object. In fact, this is just what Kant believes. The idea of God is a *heuristic* principle, a principle by which we conduct investigations, particularly investigations into morality. But this is far from establishing the objective reality of a corresponding entity. As Kant says, "This idea serves merely to indicate a certain unobtainable perfection, and limits the operations of the understanding rather than extends its sphere by the presentation of new objects."

Kant's belief that the idea of God is a heuristic or methodological principle does not follow validly from the thesis that necessary concepts may correspond to no objective reality. The question still remains open; and Kant proceeds to his demolition of the ontological argument.

Kant accuses the rationalists, in their talk about a necessary being, of never stopping to inquire how it is possible even to think about such a being, not to mention proving its existence. "A verbal definition of the concept is certainly easy enough: it is something, the non-existence of which is impossible. But this definition does not throw any light on the conditions which make it impossible to cogitate the non-existence of anything."

Of course it is easy to state a condition which makes it impossible to cogitate the *existence* of something. If a definition is self-contradictory, there can be no corresponding object. Anselm, in fact, said this. But Kant's question concerns the condition that might make it impossible to cogitate the *non-existence* of something. What condition would prevent one from thinking that God does not exist? Toward the end of his argument Anselm contended that God so truly exists that he cannot be conceived not to exist. The reason given was, "If a mind could conceive of a being better than thee [as is easily done if *thee* is a non-existent object], the creature would rise above the Creator; and this is most absurd." As expressed, this is not a very clear reason. Doubtless it means that the statement of the fool, "There is no God," is self-contradictory and therefore false. Presumably Kant knew what Anselm had said (though one modern writer thinks that Kant had never read Anselm)*, and in that knowledge obviously believed that his own stricture was applicable: To wit, no one can state a condition that makes it impossible to cogitate the non-existence of anything.

He thought it was applicable, no doubt, because the rationalists, when pressed to explain necessity, cited geometrical examples: a triangle, they said, necessarily has three angles; to say that a three-angled figure has only two angles is self-contradictory. The trouble with this, Kant points out, lies in the fact that the example is an example of a necessary judgment; what is needed is an explanation of a necessary thing. The geometrical example does not prove that three angles necessarily exist *in it*. But the ontological argument claims to prove, not the necessity of a proposition, but the existence of an object.

Kant presses this point. "If in an identical judgment," says

---

* Arthur C. McGill, in *The Many Faced Argument*, p. 38, says, "It has recently become clear that Anselm's own work, the *Proslogion*, was not known either by Immanuel Kant or Thomas Aquinas." McGill also quotes A. Koyré, *L'Idée de Dieu*.

Kant, "I annihilate the predicate in thought, and retain the subject, the result is a contradiction; and hence I say that the former belongs necessarily to the latter. But if I suppress both subject and predicate in thought, no contradiction arises; for there remains nothing at all, and therefore no means of forming a contradiction. To suppose the existence of a triangle and not that of its three angles, is self-contradictory; but to suppose the non-existence of both triangles and angles is perfectly admissible. So it is with the concept of an absolutely necessary being. Annihilate its existence in thought, and you annihilate the thing itself with all its predicates. How then can there be any room for contradiction?"

There is a slight lack of finesse here. Maybe it is only verbal carelessness. However, the example of the triangle does not perfectly fit. The example is, A triangle has three angles. The main matter is, God has existence. Annihilate the triangle in thought and the three angles vanish automatically. But then Kant does not say, Annihilate God in thought and existence vanishes automatically. What he actually said was, Annihilate God's existence, and God vanishes. Is this only a verbal slip? He could have said (couldn't he?), Annihilate God in thought, and his existence disappears at the same time. If this is what Kant really meant, then there is another question that goes beyond verbal slips. Is it possible to "annihilate God in thought?"

What does it mean to annihilate something in thought? Does it mean merely not to think about it? Refusing to think surely is a prescription for avoiding self-contradiction, but what bearing such a refusal has on God, or even on angles, is hard to say. Maybe then annihilation means denial of existence. If I positively deny that there are any triangles, it is not absurd to deny triangularity. If now I positively deny that God exists, it is not absurd to deny his existence. But this does not fit the triangle example. With respect to triangles Kant had insisted that the denial of the subject eliminates the predicate. But when Kant turns to the main matter and demands, Deny God exists; he asks us to deny, not the subject as in the triangle example, but the predicate. Thus his argument does not hang together. If now Kant retreats to the notion of not-thinking God, there is a further consideration. Though it seems true that one can think, can think botany for example, without thinking angles, it is not so clear that one cannot think God. A rationalist might well say, if a thinker thinks anything, he must think God. Augustine, recall, showed not only that truth was possible; he showed truth was inevitable and inescapable. If we think at all, we think the laws of logic. Truth is inherent or innate in the mind. But God is truth. Therefore it is impossible to annihilate God in thought. He exists so truly that he cannot even be conceived not to exist.

Kant was aware of this. He specifically referred to it. Here is what he wrote: "You find yourselves compelled to declare: There are certain subjects which cannot be annihilated in thought. But this is nothing more than saying, There exist subjects which are absolutely necessary—the very hypothesis which you are called upon to establish."

Where does this leave us now? The argument back and forward has lived up to its reputation of being extremely complicated and subtle. It seems to be a subject particularly inappropriate for a student who has had little or no philosophy. Yet how can a philosophy of religion avoid discussing the existence of God? Atheism may in a sense be called a religion; but colloquially and in common opinion if there be no God, there can be no religion. The student is into it now; turning back would be cowardice or laziness. He must therefore suffer on. Perhaps, just perhaps, it will get easier.

Where then does the argument, pro and con, leave us? There are three things Kant cannot claim to have done. First, it may be true to say that the assertion "there are certain things that cannot be annihilated in thought," is equivalent to the proposition, "there exist subjects which are absolutely necessary." But if the rationalist is called upon to substantiate this assertion, then Kant should also make clear what he means by annihilating something in thought and should show that God can be so annihilated. The situation is pretty much of a draw. In fact, Kant has a little the worse of it, for Augustine and Anselm at least tried to substantiate their view, but Kant has done nothing to show how God can be annihilated in thought.

In the second place he cannot claim to have disproved the existence of God. In fact, he himself insists that no one can disprove God's existence, for if, as he believes, all the arguments for God's existence are invalid, it still might be true that God exists. But in the third place, he cannot legitimately claim at this point that he has disproved the ontological argument. At most he has shown that the argument is incomplete. He might say that Anselm and Spinoza use as a premise the proposition they wish to establish as a conclusion. But in reply Augustine would surely say, the argument is complete, for we have shown that it is necessary to think God.

Kant still has two more points to make, two related points, maybe just one point, or at least the previous point over again.

In the early pages of his *Critique of Pure Reason* Kant distinguished between *analytic* and *synthetic* judgments. Analytic judgments are those whose predicates are logically contained in their subjects. "For example, when I say, 'all bodies are extended,' this is an analytical judgment; for I need not go beyond the conception of *body* in order to find extension connected with it, but merely analyze the conception" (p. B. 11). Synthetic judgments are *augmentative.* They are not conceptually contained in the subject, but add additional information about it. If I say, the desk is brown, the judgment is synthetic because no analysis of the meaning of the term *desk* will require this desk to be brown.

Kant now asks, Is the judgment "God exists" analytic or synthetic? If it is analytic, the predicate adds nothing to the concept of the subject. "But then the concept in your mind is identical with the thing itself," and you have proved only the existence of your concept. "But if you confess, as every reasonable person must, that every existential proposition is synthetical, how can it be maintained that the predicate of existence cannot be denied without contradiction—a property which is the characteristic of analytical propositions alone?" (p. B. 626).

The second point, that is, the same one over again, is

Being is not a real predicate, that is, a conception of something which is added to the conception of some other thing. . . . Logically it is merely the copula of a judgment. The proposition, *God is omnipotent,* contains two conceptions, . . . the word *is* is no additional predicate. . . . If I take the subject [God] with all its predicates [omnipotence being one] and say, *God is,* or, *There is a God,* I add no new predicate to the conception of God; I merely posit or affirm the existence of the subject with all its predicates—I posit the *object* in relation to my *conception.*

Then Kant continues with his famous illustration of one hundred dollars and their relation to his bank account.

Thus the real contains no more than the possible. A hundred real dollars contain no more than a hundred possible dollars. For, as the latter indicate the conception, and the former the object, on the supposition that the content of the former was greater than that of the latter, my conception would not be an expression of the whole object, and would consequently be an inadequate conception of it. But in reckoning my wealth there may said to be more in a hundred real dollars, than in a hundred possible dollars—that is, in the mere conception of them. For the real object—the dollars—is not analytically contained in my conception (which is merely a determination of my mental state), although this objective reality—this existence—apart from my conception, does not in the least degree increase the aforesaid hundred dollars.*

Two of Kant's rather enthusiastic commentators wrote, "The popularity of Kant's criticism of this argument, Hegel has remarked, results probably from his homely illustration of the one hundred dollars."† No doubt this homely, this very homely, illustration stands out like an oasis in an 884 page desert of the most crabbed literary style on record. Nevertheless, to base the reputation of a great philosopher on an illustration is rather hard on Kant. The two commentators, in spite of their admiration for Kant, continue,

> Everyone can see that in the case of the dollars you cannot deduce the being from the mere notion; but it is important to remember that the illustration is not quite apt. The very nature of a finite object is expressed by saying that its Being in time and space is discrepant from its notion. God, on the contrary, ought to be what can only be "thought as existing"; His Notion involved Being. It is this unity of the Notion and Being that constitutes the notion of God. What Kant has shown is that on the supposition that Sensibility is different in source from Understanding, you cannot infer existence in space and time from a mere concept. But Hegel saw that this supposed difference in source was a fiction; Sensibility as well as Understanding is but a phase of Thought, and so Kant's laborious argumentation here is not worth much.

There is another famous illustration. During Anselm's lifetime a monk, Gaunilo, opposed him. Gaunilo's chief point is that concepts must be constructed out of sensory materials. A merely verbal definition, such as, that than which nothing greater can be conceived, carries no meaning. Then Gaunilo

---

* *Kritik der reinen Vernunft,* B. 627.
† Mahaffy and Bernard, *Kant's Critical Philosophy,* London, 1889, p. 340.

describes his island that is the best and greatest of all possible islands. The illustration is a failure worse than Kant's. Illustrations are always dangerous.

It is now to be observed that whether one accepts the ontological argument or rejects it does not depend, does not ultimately depend on the complexities of Kant's refutation. The latter depends on a theory of knowledge in which the data of sensation are crucial. The rationalist rejects Kant's distinction between analytic and synthetic judgments. For him all truth is analytic. Therefore he refuses to be brow-beaten when Kant declares that every reasonable person must agree that existential propositions are synthetic. In fact, Kant himself is not quite able to maintain his point, for if existence is not an attribute or predicate, like the predicate brown attached to a desk, then existential judgments cannot be synthetic, for they have no predicates and are not judgments at all. Further, regardless of historical accidents and inconsistent oscillations of some timid rationalists, one can take Gaunilo by the horns and insist that "I do too have an intuition of God! And you would find yours if you only recognized what goes on when you think."

Now, before we leave the question of the existence of God and proceed to some subsidiary theorems, the idea of existence itself calls for one more remark. Kant had insisted that existential judgments are always synthetic. He had also maintained that existence is not an attribute. Suppose now that we accept this last sentence, that existence is not an attribute, and by it deny that existential judgments are synthetic. In fact, suppose we deny that there are any existential judgments. Although this may sound strange to students who have not studied much philosophy, and although it may sound insane to some philosophers who are very much enamoured of existential propositions, there is a fairly decent argument to support the contention. It is this: If a predicate can be attached to everything without exception, it has no distinct meaning, and this is to say that it has no meaning at all. If a house is *mur,* and a cat is *mur,* and a boat, a mountain, a word, a dream, are *mur,* and if beauty and justice are *mur,* and the square root of minus one as well as aleph null, it begins to become clear that *mur* has no meaning. The judgment that a house is tall makes sense only because cats and some other things are not tall. If beauty and justice are norms, the assertion makes sense only because some subjects are not norms. That is to say, a predicate that attaches to everything without exception has no meaning. Here then is the conclusion: The predicate existence can be attached to everything real or imaginary without exception. Dreams exist, mirages exist, the square root of minus one exists. These statements, however, are meaningless; they tell us nothing about dreams and the square root of minus one. What we want to know is how one thing differs from another. Why is a dream not the square root of minus one; why is a house not a cat? Similarly the question that needs to be asked about God is not whether he exists, but what he is. Of course God exists. Anything exists, so far as the term has any faint meaning at all. But it makes a great difference whether God is a dream, a mirage, or the square root of minus one. Spinoza did not need to prove that God exists. His important point was that God is the universe. But if God is not the universe, if, contrariwise, God is the Creator and Judge of all mankind, then we are dealing with substantial questions instead of non-sense syllables like existence.

Subsidiary Theorems

From what has gone before with its seeming defense of the ontological argument, someone will jump to the conclusion that rationalism, even if not the same in method with dogmatism, generally arrives at the same conclusions. This was undoubtedly true of Anselm, and of Augustine so far as he followed the rationalistic method. But there is nothing historically necessary in this connection. Spinoza was no defender of the orthodox faith, Jewish or Christian. Nor were some others. Examples now follow. These examples will show that modern rationalism is generally antagonistic toward Christianity. They will also show that the philosophy of religion is not narrowly restricted to the existence of God. The religiously inclined student agreed at the beginning of this book that whatever the definition of religion might turn out to be, it would certainly include something about God. He also agreed that a proof of God's existence was an important part of the general subject. But as the discussion passed beyond Anselm to Kant, religion seemed to evaporate into an epistemological mist. The subsidiary theorems, now to be considered, return us to distinctly religious material. It may be anti-religious material, but it is religious subject matter. The first example concerns the very foundation of dogmatism and of Christianity, namely, revelation.

Dogmatism accepts revelation as it is. It then attempts to systematize it and draw out its unexpressed implications. Rationalism, on the other hand, does not accept an alleged revelation as written. It tests the document's claim to be a revelation. This test consists in determining whether the contents of the document (the Bible) are such that God could have revealed; for rationalism believes that it can deduce by its own method what God can and cannot say.

With this procedure rationalism may turn out to have no revelation at all. The twentieth-century humanist, Edwin A. Burtt, in his (seven or more) *Types of Religious Philosophy* (first edition pp. 451 ff.) summarizes an argument that has been built up over some time.

If human intelligence, so the argument runs, is inherently defective, in that it cannot of itself discover all that a man needs for his own ultimate good, how can intelligence be trusted to prove the mere existence of God, without whom there could be no revelation? Conversely, if the mind is competent to prove God's existence, then why can it not continue and deduce everything necessary for salvation? Then revelation would be superfluous.

Burtt's words are, "If the human mind is intrinsically competent, then given time and appropriate experience, it can presumably solve all problems itself and needs no revelation from a superhuman mind; if it is not intrinsically competent, then is it not likely to be mistaken in drawing the conclusion that supernatural aid is available?" (p. 452).

Then he adds,

> If a man's reason is competent to tell that God's goodness implies the provision of a supernatural revelation, it needs no such revelation, being able to decide equally well what man's own attainment of good requires; if it is incompetent to point the way to human salvation, it is still more incompetent to conclude anything about infinite providence—the latter may be entirely incomparable with our finite ideas of good and may disappoint all the expectations which they would lead us to entertain (p. 454).

This is a very fine statement of an argument found in many authors and often in poorer form. It seems to be quite convincing to its advocates; and since its advocates are numerous, time is not wasted in reproducing a poorer form as another example. It comes from Frederick Ferré.*

Frederick Ferré

Under the sub-head *Justifying Our Enterprise* Ferré discusses the "theological veto." "One theological position denounces as impious the entire program of philosophy, at least when it turns its attention ... [to] the existence of God, miracles, life after death, or the like." This quotation and much of the wording on the adjoining pages is more ambiguous than Ferré and most people think. Chapter one, above, noted that

---

* *Basic Modern Philosophy of Religion,* pp. 22ff. and 96ff.

Gilson asserted that Calvinism makes philosophy impossible. The reason was that Calvinism makes Thomistic philosophy impossible. But is it proper, we ask, to restrict the honorable term *philosophy* to one of its species and on that basis deny the honorableness to other views?

The same ambiguity attaches to "Our Enterprise" that Ferré wishes to justify. It should be as clear as it is true that dogmatism differs completely from other systems. Also it is both possible and praiseworthy to explain the difference. But by describing "Our Enterprise" in very comprehensive phrases, Ferré wants to show that dogmatism is a failure. Had he more precisely defined his enterprise, the failure of dogmatism would be seen to be no more dishonorable than the failure of Hegel to be Humean. Ferré defines his enterprises as "a comprehensive and critical way of thinking about religion;" but for this reason—this vague and general phrase—he cannot properly assert that dogmatism vetoes it.

Philosophy of religion is impious and impossible, according to Ferré's description of dogmatism, because of "the utterly depraved status of mankind. . . . To judge of divine matters (it is said) with human reason is to proclaim reason sovereign rather than God. . . . Even arguing by reason in defense of the certitudes of faith shows faithlessness, since it presupposes—in practice—the faith *needs* the defense of reason, i.e. that God can be *benefitted* by the dialectical strategems of our minds."

Have there ever been any dogmatists who held such a view? Luther indeed held that men's faculties were all depraved. But as a disciple of Occam he did not use depravity as a refutation of Thomas. Adam before the fall could not have constructed a valid cosmological argument for the existence of God. The trouble lies not in man's mind, depraved or innocent, but in the lack of premises. The usual dogmatist position is that the world as a whole, with man's mind in it, does not have any resources from which those premises can be obtained. Thomas' bifurcated view is an evidence or example of this. Although he insists on the cosmological argument, he admits that the universe does not contain premises from which the doctrine of the Trinity could be deduced. It is not that man is sinful, depraved, at enmity with God (however important this is in other respects); it is simply that the premises are not available. This that Thomas does with half of his position, the dogmatist in consistency applies completely.

Perhaps there has been one man to whom Ferré's words apply; though whether he is a dogmatist or not is a further question.

Ferré seems to think that Karl Barth held the position described under the theological veto; at least he quotes him. Now, there may be difficulties in interpreting Barth; but one thing is clear about both Barth and Brunner. They deny logic itself and contend that we must believe paradoxes, *i.e.,* contradictory propositions.* Barth makes a point of condemning all argument for natural theology as fallacious; but certainly this point is paradoxical in an author who considers it very religious to accept fallacious paradoxes. However, if Ferré has chiefly in mind Barth and the dialectical theologians, the traditional dogmatists, who never thought of denying logic, cannot be included under the theological veto. And as for benefitting God, that is a ridiculous notion.

However interpretations of Barth may vary, and regardless of whether Ferré can find accurate examples of his description, it is fitting to consider how he proceeds to veto the veto. "First, the veto is futile. It rests on the impossible supposition that reason *can,* even in theory, be isolated from 'matters of faith.' In fact, the very intent to make intelligible use of language . . . commits one at a minimum to reason's rule of consistency."

Ferré is absolutely right in insisting that intelligibility,

---

* Compare Gordon H. Clark, *Karl Barth's Theological Method,* pp. 53-60. Brunner insists that faith must curb logic, that we must be inconsistent, and that God and the medium of conceptuality are mutually exclusive.

without which words would be meaningless, commits one to the laws of logic. This point is utterly destructive of Barth, Brunner, *et al.* As Ferré well notes, to issue the veto itself is to use logic. And if this is what the veto means, without some connotation being smuggled in, it shows decisively that the veto is futile. It does not show, however, that Ferré's argument against the veto does not apply to traditional dogmatists—not even to Tertullian in spite of some vigorous language. For while Tertullian surely held that Christian doctrine seemed impossible and absurd to the non-Christian mind, neither he nor any other traditional dogmatist held that revelation is meaningless. Indeed dogmatists vigorously assert that their doctrines are true and that the contradictories are false. In this they are devoutly committed to "reason." Here, however, is the difficulty. Ferré's argument, if it seems plausible, depends on an ambiguous use of the word *reason.* Ferré first uses this term to mean *logic* and then switches to the meaning *natural theology.* His argument against Barth is sound because Barth is illogical, even anti-logical, not because of a denial of natural theology. Traditional dogmatists deny natural theology, but they do not repudiate logic. That Ferré confuses the two meanings and tries to apply his argument to a logical as well as to the anti-logical veto, transferring the probability, indeed the certainty, of the latter to the former, is seen in his quotation from Barth, which begins, "If you really reject natural theology, . . ." But there is no inconsistency in being committed to logic and at the same time denying the validity of some or all rationalistic deductions.

Credit Ferré with a fleeting recognition of the logical situation. He says (p. 24), "The veto, let us admit at once, is logically irrefutable." So it is. Dogmatism is based on the principle of revelation. From that principle it deduces what it can. Rationalism is based on the principle of anti-revelation. From that principle it deduces what it can. But neither dogmatism nor logic will accept a theorem of rationalism, no matter how validly drawn, as a refutation. The theorem is supererogatory, for revelation was already rejected, but not refuted, in the first principle. Ferré says nearly as much. At the end of his argumentation he concludes (p. 26),

> These remarks will not, certainly, convert an ardent defender of the theological veto. He has made a basic religious value judgment that leaves the claims of philosophic thinking [again the dishonorable propaganda] relatively low on his scale of priorities. . . . If he cares to continue thinking further with us . . . he may conclude that we are profoundly mistaken, but in the process his horizons will have been extended to include new possibilities. And this too, is a worthy goal of philosophy.

These last few lines are not humility; they are arrogance and conceit, comparable with two other of his "arguments," one accusing the dogmatists of bigotry and the other accusing them of pride.

On a later page (p. 97) Ferré comes closer to Burtt's better statement. "A dilemma looms," he says. "Either the evidence [for the authenticity of the revelation] is *independent* of the alleged revelation, in which case revelation is not the *unique* path to religious knowledge . . . or else the evidence is *dependent* on the proposed authority itself, and the revelation fails, in consequence, to win its credential as a *reasonable* source of trustworthy propositions" (italics his).

The two parts of this dilemma need separate treatment. The second part is by far the more important one, but the first contains an added complication that should not be ignored. Taken very literally the first part is tautologically true: If *all* religious knowledge comes by revelation, of course there can be *none* that is independent. Augustine, however, who was a sort of dogmatist, held that while only in revelation can one learn of the Atonement (on this point Thomas Aquinas agrees also), yet there is external evidence to show that the Bible is indeed a divine revelation. The situation is similar to the procedure of law courts in evaluating witnesses. Evidence given in many ways convinces the jurors that the witness supplies information that no one else possesses. Similarly Peter and Paul, and Isaiah too, showed their sincerity by enduring severe persecution over a long period of time. When they then tell us that God revealed certain information to them, we must believe them.* But the theological veto still holds because there is no other way to discover this information. God alone can reveal that he justifies believers by means of their faith on the basis of Christ's righteousness. No observation of nature can tell us that. Ferré's criticism therefore does not apply even to Augustine. One may criticize Augustine for being an inconsistent dogmatist, an inconsistent rationalist, for permitting some sensory knowledge, for accepting too much from the Neoplatonists, or whatever else comes to mind, but not because he used the theological veto. In particular, the critics argue fallaciously when they say, if man is competent to discover one truth, he is competent to discover all truth and needs no revelation.

The second half of the disjunction was: "or else the evidence is *dependent* on the proposed authority itself, and the revelation fails, in consequence, to win its credentials as a *reasonable* source of trustworthy propositions."

This disjunct faces two replies. First, it assumes that a first principle cannot be self-authenticating. Yet every first principle must be. The first principle of Logical Positivism is that a sentence has no meaning unless it can be verified (in principle at least) by sensory experience. Yet no sensory experience can ever verify this principle. Anyone who wishes to adopt it must regard it as self-authenticating. So it is with all first principles. Ferré may not be a logical positivist, but he is an empiricist of some sort. If the dogmatist or rationalist questions empiricism, Ferré can defend himself only by saying that experience proves

---

* For this argument we may omit the possibility that it was the devil and not God who made the revelation. At any rate, they did not invent the doctrines out of their own resources.

that experience alone is reasonable.

Here the word *reasonable* leads to the second criticism of this disjunct. It is vitiated by the same ambiguous use of the word *reason* that occurred in the veto argument. If the evidence for a revelation is internal, he says, the revelation lacks credentials as a *reasonable* source of trustworthy propositions. But this is just one way of saying that "reasonableness" can be had only on an anti-revelational principle. Thus as Ferré wanted to restrict the honorable term *philosophy* to one type of philosophy, he also wants to deny *reason* and *reasonable* to those who reject his first principle. The absence of external evidences, the denial of other sources of truth, clearly does not prove a document to be unreasonable in the sense of self-contradictory or meaningless. The important and substantial question therefore concerns the existence of other sources of information. The dogmatist can very well use reason against rationalism. He can try to show that the theorems of rationalism do not follow from its own principles. He can go further and try to show that religious content cannot be derived from empirical principles either. By reason he can also show, and very easily, that dogmatism implies religious propositions. But he does not need "reason" for his choice of the dogmatic principle. "Reason" gives no principles at all.

Edwin A. Burtt

Burtt's argument was a better one because it did not depend on ambiguities. A dilemma too, it examined the consequences of the mind's competency and incompetency. To summarize the quotations given earlier, the first half of the dilemma says: If the mind of man is by its structure inherently incapable of deducing all that he needs for his own ultimate good, then man could not even prove the existence of God and hence could not prove that there is a revelation. To reinforce the point: If the mind is incapable of pointing the way to salvation, it can conclude nothing about infinite providence and its expectations may be disappointed.

The invalidity of arguing that the inability to deduce theorems x, y, z presupposes the inability to deduce theorems, a, b, c has already been pointed out; but additional reasons will now be given. In the first place, a merely average high school student may be able to work through the first or second book of Euclid, but would be completely baffled to inscribe the five regular solids in the sphere. Burtt might reply that his argument is not bound to a merely average student, but relates to the mind's inherent structure. In the second half of the dilemma this point reappears in such a way that Burtt cannot evade it. In the second place, the first half of the dilemma is invalid because extra axioms may be needed. If the six theorems, a, b, c and x, y, z, all depended on the same set of axioms and on no others, Burtt's inference would be satisfactory for a mind as keen as Euclid's. But if theorems x, y, z require additional axioms, Burtt's argument fails. This, one can learn from Thomas Aquinas. The reason Thomas could not deduce the Trinity was not any inherent incompetence of the mind, but the lack of the necessary axioms. Beyond this, the wording of Burtt's dilemma leaves the dogmatist untouched. The latter is quite willing to admit that man cannot "'conclude anything about infinite providence" on non-revelational grounds, and that men's expectations are more than likely to be disappointed.

Is the second half of Burtt's dilemma any better? It said, if the mind is competent, time and experience will solve all problems, and no revelation will be necessary. Check with the quotations a few pages back, or better, read Burtt's book.

The expressed conclusion is, No revelation is needed. The high school student will eventually inscribe the solids. Burtt himself realizes that there is a complicating circumstance. He tried to take care of it by supposing that a man had sufficient time to figure out all the theorems, that he had "experience" enough to discover the premises, and, Burtt should have added, had intelligence enough to carry through the deductions. But no man has sufficient time to solve all problems; even on optimistic assumptions it is not likely that any man has sufficient experience; and it is surely the case that some men are not very intelligent. For these reasons it does not follow that no revelation is needed. Anselm had already noted that even though all the contents of the Bible could be deduced without appeal to revelation, God had compassion on the stupid peasants (or words to that effect) and gave them the saving information.

Aside from this practical consideration, the main point is the objection's irrelevancy to dogmatism. The objection is irrelevant because it is a tautology. Its premise is: If the mind is competent. . . ." One must always remember that *competent* means *without revelation.* But it is mere tautology to say that if the mind needs no revelation, it needs no revelation. Burtt is not always careful to make explicit precisely what type of incompetency he means. The reader therefore may unwittingly think of a different type, such as: incompetent to produce a valid syllogism, incompetent to reason. Dogmatism does not assert man's inability to construct valid syllogisms. It most assuredly asserts man's inability to deduce theological content from non-revelational material. Therefore the dilemma is without force.

Revelation

The first part of this chapter, because of historical accidents, pictured dogmatism and rationalism as essentially agreed on the content of traditional theology, though substantially at variance on method. The second part of this chapter showed how modern rationalists discarded the Christian contents. But the analysis of their arguments pointed out serious flaws in them; it tended to let the old conclusions stand; and it even allowed dogmatism to emerge unscathed. What now follows will not reverse the force of the analysis. The aim is to give further instances of modern rationalism's rejection of historic Christianity. The subject will remain revelation; it may even exemplify Burtt's contentions concerning the competency of "reason"; but it takes the form of deciding what revelation must be. The interest is not merely historical. It is also substantial. Anselm never dreamed that rational argument could contradict what the Bible says. For him the Bible must first be accepted as any dogmatist would accept it. Credo ut intelligam. Belief comes first; understanding follows.* For the modern rationalists understanding comes first and belief is unnecessary. They claim to have demonstrated by logic alone both the existence and nature of God. With this knowledge they can test whether a document is or is not revelation because, apart from the document, they already know what God can and cannot reveal.

One of the best historical examples is the post-Kantian Fichte. Inspired by the moral theory of his master he wrote *An Attempt at a Critique of All Revelation* (1792). His theory is that the nature of God is entirely determined by the moral law as expounded by Kant. Religion therefore consists solely in moral duties. Anything that conflicts with these principles cannot be a divine revelation. Therefore, and the *therefore* is important, no revelation could have been given unless there was a moral necessity for it at the time of its publication. No revelation can urge obedience by any prospect of future rewards and punishments, for Kant has proved that the only moral motive is

---

* As the word *competent* was ambiguous, so too the word *understanding* must be defined and understood. Anselm's use of the word did not refer to grasping the meaning of some theological proposition. It is impossible to believe what cannot be understood in this sense. A series of nonsense syllables is not an object of faith or belief. When Anselm says, credo ut intelligam, he means that first a person hears a thesis of the gospel and when the idea has entered his mind, he tries to deduce this thesis by logic alone. A high school student may be told that a triangle whose sides are three, four, and five inches is a right triangle, and he understands the words; but them, if he be a Euclid or Pascal, he tries to deduce it from axioms. This is understanding, as Anselm meant it.

reverence for the moral law. Nor can a document be a divine revelation if it contains any information attainable by natural reason. This last may seem puzzling, for Fichte certainly wants ethical duties inculcated in a revelation, and these are fully derived from Kant. Probably Fichte wants to exclude physics and history. These points are no different and hardly more explicit than Kant's *Religion Within the Limits of Mere Reason*. In fact, when Fichte's book appeared without the name of its author, everybody thought that it was Kant's. Kant's acknowledgment that not he, but a young man by the name of Fichte wrote it, made Fichte famous. But the theory is Kant's, and it was Kant who tried to rescue Psalm 59 from history for revelation by allegorically interpreting David's enemies as his evil passions.

After all the arguing back and forth it is time to end the chapter with some conclusions that will be, hopefully, neither ambiguous nor invalidly drawn. One such conclusion is that different questions may overlap. Their discussion utilizes the same material. Nevertheless their answers must be different. Is there a God, is there a revelation, is the method of dogmatism defensible, is rationalism possible—these are examples. The bare assertion of God's existence does not imply either dogmatism or rationalism, nor does it decide for or against revelation. The acceptance of rationalism, historically, did not preclude either Christianity, pantheism, or perhaps atheism. Each question must be answered, if not separately and without reference to the others, nevertheless singly and definitely.

The second conclusion is that the substantial questions are decisive. It is profitable for a student to canvass all pertinent material, more or less at random. It is essential to collect and understand the several positions. But there is nothing that takes the place of the answers to the substantial questions: Is rationalism possible? Can the existence of God be proved? Is there a revelation and how do we know it? But textbooks often postpone substantial questions; and since empiricism is a method separate from the other two, and since the existence of God is a substantial question, the next chapter will consider the third method.

III

EMPIRICISM

There are two types of philosophy of religion based on experience. The major type, from Aristotle to the present, claims to prove the existence of God on the basis of sensory data. The second type is either satisfied with an inarticulate mysticism or tries to analyze a minimum of theology out of its emotions. Some thinkers of this type—they should really be called anti-thinkers—posit a "religious experience" that is neither intellectual, sensory, nor even emotional. Perhaps the best name for this experience is "hunch"; but for purposes of study emotion seems to be a suitable classificatory term.

Sensation, however, gives the appearance of being more public and less subjective. Two or more people can see the same streak of lightning and hear the same clap of thunder. This possibility for common verification is an advantage denied to mysticism and romanticism. Moreover this method of philosophy basks in the prestige of astounding scientific advances. If science can put men on the moon, then the scientific method can prove the existence of God, if perchance there exists a God to be proved.

Aristotle and Thomas

Thomas Aquinas (1225-1274), rejecting the rationalism of Augustine and Anselm, completely altered the philosophy of the Roman Catholic church by making Aristotelianism its foundation. Book VIII of Aristotle's *Physics,* based of course on the conclusions of the seven preceding Books, is history's first instance of a detailed empirical proof of God's existence.

Thomas Aquinas' argument is history's second. There are only minor differences between them. Since Anselm's *Ontological* Argument was quoted in full, the first of Thomas's five *Cosmological* Arguments, will also be quoted.

> The first and more manifest way is the argument from motion. It is certain, and evident to our senses, that in the world some things are in motion. Now whatever is moved is moved by another, for nothing can be moved except it is in potentiality to that towards which it is moved; whereas a thing moves inasmuch as it is in act. For motion is nothing else than the reduction of something from potentiality to actuality. But nothing can be reduced from potentiality to actuality, except by something in a state of actuality. Thus that which is actually hot, as fire, makes wood, which is potentially hot, to be actually hot, and thereby moves and changes it. Now it is not possible that the same thing should be at once in actuality and potentiality in the same respect, but only in different respects. For what is actually hot cannot simultaneously be potentially hot; but it is simultaneously potentially cold. It is therefore impossible that in the same respect and in the same way a thing should be both mover and moved, *i.e.,* that it should move itself. Therefore whatever is moved must be moved by another. If that by which it is moved be itself moved, then this also must needs be moved by another, and that by another again. But this cannot go on to infinity, because then there would be no first mover, and, consequently, no other mover, seeing that subsequent movers move only inasmuch as they are moved by the first mover; as the staff moves only because it is moved by the hand. Therefore it is necessary to arrive at a first mover, moved by no other; and this everyone understands to be God.

Concerning this argument five points are to be made. In the first sentence one notices the empiricism: "It is certain and evident to our senses" that something is in motion. Unlike Augustine Thomas does not admit innate ideas or intellectual intuitions. All knowledge must be abstracted out of our sensations. Etienne Gilson, *The Philosophy of St. Thomas Aquinas* (Eng. tr. by Edward Bullough, p. 42) has a well written section neatly characterizing Augustine's position, reporting Thomas' repudiation of it, and stating the later scholar's basic empiricism.

> The postulate on which they [Augustine's and Anselm's arguments] are based is that we could have no idea either of God, or of a subsistent truth . . . unless these ideas had been implanted in us by God, or rather unless they were that very being and that very truth shared in a finite mode by our human understanding. On such an hypothesis the *a priori* proofs cannot provide any transition from the idea to being; for it is being which is the starting-point of the argument.* Underlying St. Thomas' criticisms, however, we find an entirely different postulate, namely that all our knowledge originates from sensory intuitions."

Since the simpler modern form of the cosmological argument is equally based on sensation, the first point of criticism, *i.e.*, the postulate just named, will be postponed until after the exposition of Hume's material.

The second point is one that cannot be satisfactorily canvassed in a book of this type and size. But the main criticism can be indicated with complete clarity. Aristotle's argument in Book VIII of the *Physics* depends not only on the seven preceding Books, but also on still prior logic and epistemology. Similarly Thomas' argument, just quoted, is more a summary than an argument. It too depends on long series of syllogisms. For one thing the argument uses the concepts of potentiality and actuality as well as the definition of motion that requires them. But potentiality, by which motion is defined, is itself

---

* Gilson might have noted here, had he been defending Anselm, that Kant failed to question the necessity of such a transition.

exemplified and explained (though not formally defined) by motion itself (nor is it defined in any way). For another thing, the arguments about one thing's being moved by another, and how animals do not really move themselves, are fairly intricate. And there is much more. A student who is extremely interested can occupy some months or even years digging it all out. To prove God's existence, therefore, one must make sure that every one of a thousand syllogisms is valid. If even one syllogism in the chain collapses, the whole argument is invalid. Now, it is likely, it is even probable that a flaw occurs here and there. The use of the concept of potentiality is one example. The concerned student is urged to search for others. Thus he will convince himself that Aristotle's proof of God's existence is invalid.

The third criticism is that the conclusion itself occurs as one of the premises of the argument. Thomas says, "If that by which it is moved be itself moved, then this also must be moved by another again. But this cannot go on to infinity because then there would be no first mover, and consequently no other mover, seeing that subsequent movers move only inasmuch as they are moved by the first mover." But this that is given as a reason against infinite regress (and a refutation of infinite regress is essential to the completion of the argument) is itself the conclusion, viz., there must be a first mover. This makes the argument invalid by reason of circularity.

The fourth criticism is a more difficult one and requires some introductory explanation. Aristotle had noted that an adjective or predicate, attached to two different subjects, does not always have precisely the same meaning. For example, the adjective *medical* does not mean exactly the same thing when one says "this man is a medical man," as it means when one says "this book is a medical book." There is, however, a relationship between them, in that in one way or another they both refer to the science of medicine. This relationship is called analogy. The two meanings of the term are analogical.

Thomas developed the theory of analogy far beyond the simple observation of Aristotle, and it took on major proportions when the subject was God. Thomas held that the simplicity of the divine being required God's existence to be identical with his essence. This is not the case with a book or pencil. *That* a book is and *what* a book is are two different matters. But with God existence and essence are identical.

For this reason an adjective predicated of God and the same adjective predicated of man are not univocal in meaning. One may say, God is good, and one may say, This man is good; but the predicate has two different meanings. There is no term, not a single one, that can be predicated univocally of God and of anything else.

What is true of these adjectives is also true of the verb is, or existence. In fact it is the nature of God's existence that makes the adjectives analogical. God's essence and God's existence are identical; hence existence for God means something different from existence for man. In the case of Aristotle's medical man and medical book, though the two instances are not strictly univocal, yet the medical science to which they both relate is the same science. Here there is a univocal point of reference. But for Thomas there is no such point, for no term whatever has the same meaning for God that it has for man. If some area were common to both meanings (as the science of medicine in Aristotle), then this common area could be given a name and univocally predicated of God and man. But nothing is univocally predicated. Therefore existence means one thing for God but a completely different thing for man. Thomas still calls this analogy, but it is an analogy without any univocal basis.

This is another reason why his proof of God's existence is invalid. His premises speak of the existence of moving things, hot things, etc., but the conclusion speaks of God's existence. However, for an argument to be valid the concepts in the conclusion must appear in the premises.

The fifth criticism is one that has been expressed, perhaps

somewhat timidly, by several theologians at various times, but more recently and very vigorously by Karl Barth. The last line of Thomas' proof reads, "And this everyone understands to be God." Barth replies: And this very few people understand to be God; in particular no Christian understands that Aristotle's first mover is the God of Abraham, Isaac, and Jacob. It will not do to prove the existence of some kind of first principle. Indeed there is no point in defending the necessity of a first principle of some sort. On this there is universal agreement. The important point is to determine what sort of first principle there is. If, now, Thomas' argument had validly proved the existence of Aristotle's first mover, Christianity would have been proven false. A god who has not created the world, who does not know the future and possibly not even the present and past, a god who cannot speak to men, evokes no enthusiasm from Christian thinkers. What Christianity needs is the Triune God, and Thomas (though in a sense he tries) cannot pass from the first mover to the Father, Son, and Holy Ghost. Whether an Aristotelian god would satisfy a Mohammedan, or a Buddhist, is a question left for them to answer. But the fact that several religions use the word *G-O-D* no more means that they have something in common than their use of the words *first principle.*

Paley and Hume

So much for Thomas Aquinas. Could it be that his failure was caused by the intricacy of his argument? Could it be improved by simplification? If the concept of potentiality and the theory of analogical knowledge are dropped, maybe God's existence could be proved. At any rate modern authors have used very simple arguments. Kant (not that he thinks it valid) reports one such extremely simple form: "If something exists [now], an absolutely necessary being must likewise exist." This most simple of all statements still faces Barth's objection that the conclusion never arrives at God. Other modern arguments avoid this objection and conceive of God in more traditional fashion, endowing him with intelligence, with justice, and in some cases with providential control of particular events. William Paley (1743-1805) managed to hit upon a striking illustration. If a person walks along an uninhabited beach and finds a watch on the sand, he will infer from its marvelous mechanism that an intelligent workman made it. So too the mechanism of the world implies a supernatural designer. This form of the argument is not just the bare cosmological argument based solely on the existence of something, but rather it depends on consideration of design or purpose. For this reason it is called the teleological argument.

Paley's critics* have been pretty hard on him. They complain that he paid too much attention to small details, like the structure of the eye (a strange objection to or from an empiricist) and not enough to design on a universal scale. They also complain that since no one has seen the universe as a whole, there is no observational basis for saying it is a machine like a watch. Perhaps it is alive and is more like a vegetable. These are picayune objections. Paley could have argued that the structure of a cabbage is even more intricate than that of a watch. But the basic criticisms of the cosmological argument retain their force, no matter in what form it is stated. Even the more developed form of the teleological argument is equally based on experience; and though its conclusion would be of more value to personal religion, if it is invalid, personal religion cannot appropriate its value.

The most famous set of objections to all arguments based on experience are those of David Hume (1711-1776), who analyzed them brilliantly in his *Enquiry Concerning Human*

---

* William Tennant, *Philosophical Theology*, Vol. II, pp. 84-85 (Cambridge, 1930); and J.J.C. Smart, "The Existence of God," in *New Essays in Philosophical Theology*, ed. by Antony Flew and Alasdair MacIntyre.

Understanding and his *Dialogues Concerning Natural Religion.*

In Section XI of the former work Hume outlines the teleological argument.

> The chief or sole argument for a divine existence . . . is derived from the order of nature; where there appear such marks of intelligence and design, that you think it extravagant to assign for its cause, either chance, or the blind and unguided force of matter. . . . From the order of the work, you infer, that there must have been project and forethought in the workman. If you cannot make out this point, you allow, that your conclusion fails; and you pretend not [you do not claim] to establish the conclusion in a greater latitude than the phenomena of nature will justify. These are your concessions. I desire you to mark the consequences. . . .
>
> If the cause be known only by the effect, we never ought to ascribe to it any qualities beyond what are precisely requisite to produce the effect; nor can we, by any rules of just reasoning, return back from the cause, and infer other effects from it, beyond those by which alone it is known to us.

In these lines Hume has admirably stated the logical conditions for any empirical argument. His criticisms do not apply to dogmatism or to rationalism. Neither of these methods makes any use of experience. Hume is concerned only to show the impossibility of any empirical or natural theology that still conserves some traditional religious values. To be sure, Hume was an empiricist and had no sympathy for other methods. His basic dependence on experience ruled out rationalism at the start. At this point he is solely interested in the logical value of natural theology.

Hume is willing to admit that a causal argument (if for the sake of argument there can be such a thing) might prove the existence of some sort of god or gods. They would "possess that precise degree of power, intelligence, and benevolence, which appears in their workmanship." Since their arrangements include earthquakes and tidal waves in inhabited areas, their observable benevolence is limited.

> But nothing farther can ever be proved. . . . So far as the traces of any attributes, at present, appear, so far may we conclude these attributes to exist. The supposition of farther attributes is mere hypothesis; much more the supposition that in distant regions of space or periods of time, there has been, or will be, a more magnificent display of these attributes. . . . The knowledge of the cause being derived solely from the effect, they must be exactly adjusted to each other.

Hume notes that this solves, or, better, removes the problem of evil. This ancient problem arises only on the supposition that an Almighty God desires the perfect happiness of every individual. But not only is it impossible to prove that God is omnipotent, it is impossible to prove that he has such a desire. We know him only by experience, and experience includes earthquakes. Or, more generally, *"Are there any marks of a distributive justice in the world?* If you answer in the affirmative, I conclude, that, since justice here exerts itself, it is satisfied. If you reply in the negative, I conclude, that you have then no reason to ascribe justice, in our sense of it, to the gods. . . . [Y]ou have no reason to give it any particular extent, but only so far as you see it, *at present,* exert itself."

Hume then considers the possibility that the present injustices in the world will be balanced by rewards and punishments in a heavenly consummation. Do we not, when we see a half-finished building, infer that the builder will return to finish it? Yes, we do; because we have previously seen builders return to finish half-finished buildings. It is also because we have seen builders return that we know a structure is only half-finished. But if we had never had previous experience, we could know neither that a builder would return nor that the structure before our eyes is half-finished. This is precisely our condition with respect to the world. We have never seen gods come back to finish half-finished worlds. We do not know that this present world is only half-finished. Therefore we have no reason to hope for a just, a benevolent, a heavenly consummation.

The *Dialogues Concerning Natural Religion* do not improve on the basic criticism of the *Enquiry;* in fact their tedious dialogue form is a nuisance. Nevertheless they apply the basic criticism to a few particular points, and this elucidation may prove helpful to those who consider these matters for the first time.

Near the beginning Hume asserts his fundamental empiricism. It is silly, he says, to reject Copernicus, Galileo, and Newton. Why should not belief in religion also be based on the evidence, for the methods of science and of religion are the same. If we distrust reason, we have no other principle to lead us to religion.

By these words Hume rejects dogmatism and rationalism. When he speaks of distrusting "reason," he does not mean *reason* as the rationalist understood it: He means sensory experience. Sensation is the sole source of scientific knowledge and religious belief. Nothing comes from logic alone, and there cannot be a divine revelation.

The dialogue form is not only tedious; it also enables Hume to be unclear at times. There are three personaes. Cleanthes rather obviously represents Paley and similar exponents of the cosmological argument. Philo is a sceptic, and while Hume certainly speaks through Philo, it is not certain that Hume would assert all that Philo says. Demea has been described as the inflexible defender of rigid orthodoxy. This is probably not the case. In Part X one discovers that Demea is not a dogmatist, for he makes no appeal to revelation; nor is he a rationalist, although he might seem to be in Part IX; but he is a mystic, basing his religion on his feeling of insufficiency and misery, thus anticipating Schleiermacher. And though Karl Barth does not like Schleiermacher, Demea has one idea that Barth has most prominently proclaimed. In any event Demea hardly receives fair treatment.

In answer to Cleanthes' initial assertion of the value and necessity of experience, Demea objects that everyone believes in "God." His existence need not be proved. The important question is the nature of God. *What* is God? Now, asserts Demea, human reason cannot answer this question. God is "totally other," to quote Karl Barth anachronistically. Or, more textually, the devout Malebranche said that the Spirit of God bears no resemblance to our spirit. Our ideas of wisdom, justice, and even thought, do not express what God's perfections are. Therefore our experience provides no evidence for God.

Perhaps Hume did not comment on Demea's views because he somewhat agreed. At any rate through Philo he rejects analogies based on a single case and insists that Cleanthes has no ground for saying that a world must be similar to a house or watch. We have seen houses being built; no one has seen universes originating.

If Hume does not answer Demea through Philo, he may do so through Cleanthes. After Demea, a second time, contrasts the fleeting impressions of human minds with God's immutable and incomprehensible being, Cleanthes condemns mystics and skeptics as being no better than atheists. God's mind, he says, must have ideas as distinct and as successive as men's. An immutable mind would not be a thinking, reasoning, willing mind—it would be no mind at all. God's mind must be like man's mind, "the liker the better."

Thus Cleanthes defends the empirical argument at the expense of orthodox theology, and Philo draws the conclusion that God is finite since our experience of the world is finite.

After some more argumentation Cleanthes and Philo seem to agree that the universe may be an animal or vegetable, rather than a machine, and that God is the soul of the world. In this case no external or supernatural deity is needed. Even so, how a mind produces order among its ideas is as obscure as the alleged impossibility of matter's organizing itself. Cabbages organize themselves without thinking, cannot the world do so? How can it be proved by *experience* that order requires thought? Experience shows daily that reason arises from generation, but there are no observed cases of generation arising from reason.

There are some further pages of similar material, but they are hardly necessary; nor are Kant's intricacies on the cosmological and teleological arguments. The part of Hume's material summarized is unanswerable.

Empiricism and Sensation

The discussion on these last few pages has stayed close to theology. But one must probe more deeply. Paley had assumed that he could see a watch. Hume gives the impression that he has perceived a cabbage. And does it not seem to be true that empiricism cannot get very far without some knowledge of individual objects such as these? Thomas could not begin his argument until he had seen a stone in motion. A century later William of Occam proposed an empiricism even more rigorous than that of Thomas. He insisted that reality consists only of individual objects, thus removing from the world the few remnants that Thomas had retained from Platonism. Surely empiricism must have a world of trees and stones.

Yet an empirical account of individual things is more difficult than anyone would at first expect. In the discussion of Thomas' cosmological argument, above, five criticisms were listed; but the first one, the empirical postulate itself, received no explanation. This was a serious omission, for it is impossible to judge of the complete philosophic situation without a final analysis of experience. Thomas and Hume, for all their differences in conclusions, agreed that all knowledge is based on sensation. Now, if, as most people are unwilling to admit, sensation cannot give rise to any knowledge whatever, if no laws of physics and no events of history can be so determined, if, that is, empiricism reduces to skepticism, then at least the cosmological argument does not alone crash in ruins. Empiricism as a whole crashes, and in this case rationalism becomes more plausible. Perhaps even someone might be bold enough to adopt dogmatism. Surely one cannot judge of the whole situation without a thorough-going examination of empiricism.

Such an examination is nothing new. Kant in one way and Hegel more definitely came to some negative conclusions about sensation. Malebranche, previously noted, did not neglect the subject. But above all the Greek skeptics have never been surpassed. Therefore it is strange that in this twentieth century those who show some interest in arguing in favor of God's existence, those who are relatively orthodox, pay little or no attention to theories of sensation. They stand rebuked (inferentially) by a brilliant, non-theological philosopher, Brand Blanshard, who in *The Nature of Thought* painstakingly works out a detailed theory of sensation and perception. But most conservative theologians pay no attention.

It may be of some historical interest, although his arguments are not the most profound, to see how Malebranche in the seventeenth century treated the matter. Book I, xii, 5 of his *Récherché de la Verité* goes as follows:

> These sensations are so vivid and sharp that the mind can hardly avoid attributing them to itself in some way or other. Therefore it not only concludes that they are in the objects but also that they are in parts of one's body. . . . Thus it judges that heat and cold are not only in ice and fire but that they are also in one's hands. As for weak sensations, they strike the mind so slightly that no one supposes they belong to the mind . . . nor to one's own body, but are only in the objects. For this reason we remove light and color from our minds and eyes and assign them to external objects, although science teaches us that they are not found in the definition of matter, and although also an experi-

ment shows that we should place them in the eyes as well as in the object. [The experiment consists in using the eye of a recently killed bull as a lens for a camera obscura. The colors outside will recur in the eyeball.]

... We do not know by simple eyesight, but only by reasoning, whether whiteness, light, colors, and other weak and faint sensations are or are not modifications of the mind. But as to the vivid sensations like pain and pleasure, we easily judge that they are in our minds because we so distinctly feel them striking us. . . .

In I, xiii, 5 Malebranche continues: "People think that everyone has the same sensations of the same object. We believe that everybody sees the sky as blue. . . . [But in fact people sense differently.] Sauces must be quite different to please different people, or to please the same person at different times. One likes things sweet, another likes them sour. One finds wine agreeable, another can't stand it; and the one who likes wine when he is well finds that it is bitter when he is sick."

It is clear then that sensations give us no trustworthy information about the nature of so-called external objects. Nearly everyone admits that at least some sensations are only modifications of the mind. In the eighteenth century Berkeley avoided deciding which sensations belong to the mind and which are qualities in external objects by pointing out that experiential evidence for external objects is completely lacking. In the case of any sensory object, to exist means to be perceived. Objects are sensations.

Berkeley himself did not see the skeptical thrust of empiricism. But before further modern material is given, the arguments of the ancients should be set forth. They are not to be ignored just because they are ancient.

The Greek Skeptics

Pyrrho (365-275) may be regarded as the initiator of the Hellenistic school of skeptics. Diogenes Laertius pictures him, both in his personal peculiarities and in his ability at cross-examination, as a second Socrates. The same garrulous reporter assigns to him or to his school ten causes of perplexity. The opening sentence of this passage (IX, 79, middle) is, "Perplexities arise from . . . " or, better, with an emendation, "The objections against the consistency of our percepts or concepts fall under ten heads."

The first is that living creatures do not receive the same impressions from the (allegedly) same things because some find pleasure in what others find painful. There are other differences among the sensory abilities of living beings: Hawks have keen sight, but dogs have keen smell. "It is natural that if the senses, *e.g.* eyes, of animals differ, so also the impressions produced upon them" (IX, 80).

The second head, which is only a different example of the same point, is, "Demophon, Alexander's butler, used to get warm in the shade and shiver in the sun. . . . The same ways of life are injurious to one man but beneficial to another; from which it follows that judgment must be suspended."

The third and fourth heads enumerate some conditions under which the same thing gives different impressions. Health, illness, sleep, youth, old age, heat, cold, breathing freely or with difficulty cause the impressions received to vary.

Further headings remark that purple shows different tints in sunlight, moonlight, and lamplight. A rock that takes two men to lift in air is easily moved when submerged in water, "either because, being in reality heavy, it is lifted by the water, or being light, it is made heavy by the air. Of its own inherent property we know nothing" (IX, 85). The principle behind this example is important: Nothing is seen all by itself; everything is seen in relation to other things; these relationships alter the sensation; therefore our senses do not present us with the object's inherent property. Of the object itself, we know nothing.

Would it be permissible to interrupt these ancient themes by a reference to the reader's or the writer's contemporary experience? Driving at 60 m.p.h. along a two lane highway, one sees a good sized barn a half-mile ahead on the right side. There is a small truck or bus parked in front of it. Certainly the vehicle cannot be an ordinary car, for its front end is as high as its rear. It must be a V.W. bus. Then when one has driven another two hundred feet, one sees that the bus is a mail box on a post only another hundred feet ahead, while the barn is still over two thousand feet away. Or, at night one sees several red lights ahead in the air. Are they traffic signals? Sensation cannot tell. One must organize the meaningless impressions into a huge truck. But organizing is not a sensory receiving. Some attempts at organization result in tragedy. Therefore neither the sensation nor the organization is infallible.

To return to antiquity, Arcesilaus (315-240) attacked the Stoic position that there are self-authenticating sensations. Even in dreams, in drunkenness, or in insanity, the recipient of a sensation believes it to be a correct representation of an object. Later he may decide he was mistaken; but during the sensory experience he cannot distinguish it from a true sensation. Then is it possible *now* to be certain of our sensations? Obviously at any time we may be mistaken, for we do not recognize that we are dreaming, or that we are drunk, or, if we know we are ill, we do not know whether or how much the fever affects our receptivity. Put more simply: Illusions while they last are as convincing as allegedly true sensations.

Carneades (214-129) was another important skeptic; but his points about dreams and illusions, about two eggs and twins (which we cannot tell apart) add little to the argument.

Aenesidemus (between 80 B.C.-A.D. 130), like Pyrrho, summarizes the skeptical arguments under ten headings. First, the perceiving organs of animals are different from human organs. Fish and men have different reactions to water. We can say how a thing appears to us, but not what it is, since we cannot assume that our sensations are truer than those of animals.

Second, even among men there are divergent representations. Third, even the same man, the wisest man the Stoics can find, has divergent sensations at different times. Fourth, various conditions affect our sensing. It is useless to object that conditions such as illness are abnormal and that normal sensation is trustworthy, for no one can tell whether his condition is normal or not. Headings five and six also repeat Pyrrho's list. No object is ever experienced in isolation; but its surroundings change its appearances; therefore we can never know what the object itself is like.*

A Contemporary Question

These criticisms utterly demolish empiricism and all arguments similar to those of Thomas Aquinas and William Paley. Then one must ask, Why are there any empiricists today? As indeed there are. Among evangelicals one can name J. Oliver Buswell, Jr., the late Edward John Carnell, John H. Gerstner, the late Floyd E. Hamilton, Arthur F. Holmes, George I. Mavrodes, and John Warwick Montgomery.†

Among liberals of various sorts are: Thomas J.J. Altizer, R.B. Braithwaite, Edwin A. Burtt, John Dewey, Corliss Lamont, John E. Smith, F.R. Tennant, Henry N. Wieman, and John Wisdom.

In neither of these lists do all the men emphasize sensation

---

* The historical question of the relation between Pyrrho and Aenesidemus, and whether the ancient doxagraphers attributed to the former what only the latter had written out, need not be considered here. Also, omitted are (1) the remainder of Aenesidemus' extensive arguments, and (2) all of Sextus Empiricus.

† Such lists are always incomplete and often objection is made on the ground that differences are not satisfactorily acknowledged.

to the same extent. For example, John E. Smith apparently wants to replace sensation with the experience of encounter. But whether or not these men acknowledge and utilize the role of sensation, one can well ask what would be left of their constructions if they agreed with ancient Greek skeptics.

Why then are there any empiricists today? Has some great philosopher appeared in the meantime and not only demolished skepticism once for all, but also established the infallibility of sensation? If so, it must have been since Hume, for of all empiricists Hume most clearly shows not only that experience cannot prove the existence of God, but also and perhaps reluctantly that nothing whatever can be learned from experience.

Hume's Experience

From Berkeley Hume accepts the conclusion that material or so-called external bodies do not exist; and that, if they did, we could know nothing about them. The argument is as follows. Sensory experiences, such as the sensation of red, or loud, or sweet, are mental events and take place only in the mind. People often suppose that these qualities are copies of, or resemble, things external to the mind. However, it is difficult, or rather impossible, to imagine how a sensory quality can resemble anything other than a sensory quality. How can a color resemble something invisible? How can the sensation hard resemble anything intangible? Note that the alleged external objects are not perceptions. Therefore they are non-perceptible. Only perceptions are perceptible. No one has ever seen a material body. Colors are only mental events.

If someone objects that though red and sweet are mental perceptions, extension and motion are external, the reply is: No one has ever seen extension or motion unless it is a colored extension. Experience never gives us extension or motion. One never sees anything but color.

If perhaps this argument does not completely disprove the existence of non-sensory bodies, extended in space, and if someone insists that there still might be such bodies even though we have no experience of them, Berkeley and Hume reply, even so in that case no one has the remotest idea of what such bodies could be like. In particular we could never know that they are like our ideas of red and sweet. To know that one thing is like or unlike another, we must see them both and so compare them. But since no one has seen an external body, no one can compare it with the red he has seen or the hard he has touched. Empiricism therefore furnishes no knowledge of an external world, finds no evidence for its existence, and confines the mind to the mind, *i.e.*, its sensations.

Well, it confines the mind to the mind, if there be a mind. Berkeley was sure that he had a mind. Hume finds as little empirical evidence for a perceiving mind as for material bodies. We have experience of red, sweet, and hard. Has anyone ever seen, heard, or touched a mind? All experience consists of sensory ideas and their residual memory images. These come and go; they are not active, nor do they produce anything. In particular they do not perceive. Red is a perception, not a percipient. An active perceiving being is not to be found in experience.

Hume (*Treatise,* Book I, Part IV, Section VI) writes,

> There are some philosophers who imagine we are every moment intimately conscious of what we call our Self. . . . The strongest sensation, the most violent passion, say they, instead of distracting us from this view, only fix it the more intensely. . . .
>
> Unluckily all these positive assertions are contrary to that very experience, which is pleaded for them. . . . For from what impression cou'd this idea be deriv'd? . . . It must be some one impression, that gives rise to every real idea. But self or person is not any one impression, but that to which our several impressions and ideas are suppos'd to have a reference. If any impression gives rise to the idea of self, that impression must

continue invariably the same, thro' the whole course of our lives. . . . But there is no impression constant and invariable. . . . [C]onsequently there is no such idea.

For my part, when I enter most intimately into what I call *myself,* I always stumble on some particular perception or other, of heat or cold. . . . I never can catch *myself* at any time without a perception. . . .

[Selves] are nothing but a bundle or collection of different perceptions, which succeed each other with an inconceivable rapidity. . . . The mind is a kind of theatre, where several perceptions successively make their appearance. . . . There is properly no *simplicity* in it at one time, nor *identity* in different. . . . The comparison of the theatre must not mislead us. They are the successive perceptions only, that constitute the mind; nor have we the most distant notion of the place, where these scenes are represented, or of the materials, of which it is compos'd.

Accordingly empiricism, in addition to its failure to prove God's existence, also fails to prove the existence of external bodies and internal selves.

Brand Blanshard, an Exception

Although most contemporary authors, especially religious authors, shut their eyes to the defects of empiricism, Brand Blanshard, in his two volumes on *The Nature of Thought,* makes a detailed and profound attempt to arrive at knowledge through perception. Professor Blanshard, perhaps the most brilliant American philosopher of this century, is no Humean empiricist; but no one else supplies empiricists with a better defense of their starting point. Concerning the remainder of his work this discussion has nothing to say.

The simplest form of truth, according to Blanshard, is perception. Note carefully his definition. "Perception is that experience in which, on the warrant of something given in sensation at the time, we unreflectingly take some object to be before us." This definition assumes the occurrence of sensation prior to the perception. Sensation *gives* something. It furnishes *data.* Perception, apparently, *gives* nothing. It is an action by which we *take,* suppose, or conclude that there is some object before us. The wording seems to indicate that there is no truth or knowledge in sensation, for perception is its simplest form. Nonetheless sensation issues a warrant by which we are warranted to conclude that there is an object.

This means, and Blanshard emphasizes the point, that perception is an *inference.* This raises the questions, (1) Is there a describable method by which we pass from sensation to perception? (2) Is the inference valid? and, underlying these, (3) What is sensation, if indeed there is such a thing?

Blanshard's answer to the third question is very honest, very enlightening, but perhaps not very complete. He candidly admits that "the reconstruction of a preperceptual" state of mind, which occurs only in infants because later in life perception is never absent, "has peculiar dangers." Among these dangers are these two. First, we are in danger of reading back into sensation elements of perception. Second, if we avoid this first danger, we are likely to reconstruct a state of mind, if it can be called a state of mind, so simple that escape from it into perception is inconceivable.

Unfortunately Blanshard never defines sensation—except as "the nether limit of perception," and this is of no use in constructing a theory. After studying the first seventy-five pages of the volume, one begins to wonder whether there is any such thing as sensation. A nether limit, from which we cannot escape, or at least about which we know nothing, is not a satisfactory basis for a system of philosophy.

There is a second point, possibly more easily apprehended by those who are not yet ready to deny the existence of sensation. Blanshard with indefatigable patience shows how one might infer a peception. In this he displays great psychological acuity; and beholding his intricate analyses is a high aesthetic experience. However, there is one thing missing. Let him assume his warrant from sensation, let him show how the inference of perception is actually made, I do not see that he anywhere shows that the inference is valid. Upon the warrant of a blue sensation we take a silk dress to be before us. This we do. But people make all sorts of invalid inferences, both within and beyond perception. To explain perception as an inference is one thing; to show which if any, of these inferences is valid, is another thing; and this is what was needed to save empiricism.* Poor empiricists: Not only is God gone, sensation and perception are gone too!

Memory

It is unnecessary to kill a corpse many times over, but some interest attaches to the vagaries of memory. Suppose it were possible to know that a book was there, even if *there* means in the mind. This knowledge would be entirely useless unless we could use it at a later time. No matter how certain the book at the moment, the book must remain in our mind, if we are to extend and develop our understanding. The book must become the foundation for further knowledge. Now, the day after I certainly perceive the book, I remember I saw a book with a blue binding (for I could not perceive a book without color). The day after that I remember that the book was brown. How can I decide at this later date what it was I so surely perceived some time earlier? How is it possible to certify the accuracy of memory?

An unsuspecting empiricist might say: Go look at the book again and see. This answer presupposes first that the book was not merely in the mind but was an external object; and this

---

* If Blanshard can save himself through his Hegelianism, then he is a sort of rationalist. But the discussion here envisages empiricism only.

presupposition according to the preceding argument can no longer be made. But besides this, in the second place, if we go look and see, we depend on our memory that we are now looking at the same book we looked at two days ago. Thus we are assuming the trustworthiness of memory to prove which of two contradictory memories is correct.

Why then are there any empirical philosophers? Or, at least, why, in the face of these annihilating objections, does anyone try to base religion on experience and ignore, or refuse to answer, the arguments of their opponents?

Religious Experience

If some guesswork is allowed, one reason empirical philosophers of religion do not face their opponents on these basic matters is their belief that sensation is of no religious use because there is a "religious experience" that satisfies all requirements.

If this guess is more or less accurate, it ought to be said first of all that religious experiences are more doubtful than sensory experiences. These gentlemen, in my opinion, have not carefully enough considered the logical effects of sensory skepticism on their position. If blue books are doubtful, and memory too, what can be had from emotional upheavals? As empiricists they are under obligation to explain sensation, even if only to attempt to divorce it from religion. Suppose the religious experience is that of fear. It cannot be fear of the dark, or of a dim grizzly-bear shape in the dark, for these are sensations. Is a religious fear then a fear of nothing? One may further ask, does religion have any relationship to the world in which we live? Of course, the answer could be negative. And this opens vistas upon the vast non-existent. But if the answer is affirmative, as it usually is, then to explain the relationship the empiricist must defend some view of the world. To do so, if he still continues to be an empiricist, what can he use without sensation?

However, though his unwitting dependence on sensation must be pressed against the incautious emotionalist, there is another objection that adherents of this viewpoint will see is more immediate and direct. The objection is that analysis of religious experience fails to arrive at any religious conclusions.

Aside from mystics, who have occurred throughout history in small numbers, the vogue of religious experience in modern times began with Schleiermacher. For him, whatever can be said about religion—Schleiermacher had theological statements in mind—is to be obtained by analyzing the experience. He identified the experience as the feeling of absolute dependence. Later authors have modified this identification somewhat, but the methodology remains the same and the analysis produces no results.

H.N. Wieman, in a sense, remains close to Schleiermacher. He defines God as those characteristics of the universe from which we obtain the greatest goods and by which we avoid the worst evils. This definition, which reduces God to several parts of the universe, is based on a feeling of dependence, even if not the absolute dependence of Schleiermacher. The defensible contents of religion must then be made to conform to this experience.

Professor Smith

John E. Smith, Professor of Philosophy at Yale University, is farther removed from Schleiermacher and is even violently, well, very vigorously opposed to sensory empiricism. For both these reasons he is a good example of non-Humean empiricists. It is essential of course to explain what he means by experience.

Smith begins his rejection of earlier empiricism with the sentence:

It is often said by theologians that an analysis starting with the universal fact of religion involves us in a morass of subjectivity and forces us to depend entirely upon purely human experience. . . . They are too willing to accept an outmoded conception of what it is and means. . . . The philosophical standpoint required for this task is that of radical empiricism, making central the doctrine that experience is an objective and critical product of the intersection between reality in all its aspects on the one hand and a self-conscious being capable of receiving that reality through significant form on the other. . . . Despite much talk of "empiricism" in modern philosophy, actual experience in its full range and depth has frequently been ignored. . . .*

From the time of Aristotle to the present the term *experience* has indeed been used to designate a full range and depth of the intersection between reality and a self-conscious being. One must not quarrel about this linguistic usage. Aristotle spoke of *experienced* carpenters and musicians. The trouble, however, lies in explaining how such people became experienced. They were not born that way. They had to practice. They had to begin with something much more simple than experience in this sense of the term. Therefore, if one is an empiricist, there must be an "experience" otherwise defined. Smith speaks of a "critical product of the intersection between reality in all its aspects on the one hand and a self-conscious being capable of receiving that reality." How is such a being capable? What is the method of receptivity? Is there any evidence of a reality that can intersect with a self-conscious being? What does intersection mean? A philosopher who complains that other philosophers have "ignored" the full range of experience should not ignore the problem of explaining how a "critical product" is produced.

---

* *Experience and God* (New York: Oxford University Press, 1968), p. 11.

Smith ignores the problem of explanation; he does not ignore the earlier empiricism that made a brave attempt. Only, he does not think the attempt brave or successful.

> There have been, for example, narrow theories of experience that would confine it to data supposedly disclosed through the senses . . . atomic data exclusive of relations. . . . The chief obstacles that have hindered the development of an adequate theory of experience in modern philosophy are these: First, many philosophers have assumed that experience is a "mental" product . . . in the consciousness of the individual (pp. 22-23).

Yet Smith himself posited a self-conscious receptive being. Is not even the full range and depth of a carpenter's "experience" mental, conscious, and indeed subjective? How much more subjective must be the experiences out of which the carpenter critically constructs his product!

Therefore must not a careful thinker reject as plainly false Smith's assertion that, "In the most basic sense, experience is a many-sided product of complex encounters between what there is and a being capable of . . . responding to and expressing it"? Surely this cannot be the most basic sense of experience. Encounters in the plural cannot be more basic than the first encounter in the singular. There must be something that precedes the "critical product." Must not the self-conscious being respond to this more elementary X? And if it is the response of a self-conscious being, must not the experience be mental? Without such a mental event how can the responding, receptive being learn "what is there"?

But no. "The chief error of taking experience as 'mental' or 'subjective' consists in the uncritical assumption that experience is a record or report to be found entirely within the mind . . ." (p. 24). Smith rejects this because it leads to subjective idealism and therefore to skepticism. Since this result makes him feel uncomfortable, he refuses to explain how a non-mental experience can teach a conscious being that there is an external reality.

Furthermore, if "experience" is a product of two factors, a stone and a person, then each equally has the experience. The experience belongs to the stone quite as much as it belongs to the person. Then is the stone also a self-conscious being? If, on the other hand, the experience does not belong to both in the same way, the person must have something the stone does not have; and is not this something a subjective mental experience that leads the person to think that what he sees is a stone?

Indeed Smith cannot avoid these embarrassments. He acknowledges that "experience is much more than a *reflection* or mirror image of what is encountered. The one who experiences *refracts* as well as *reflects*. . . . The total nature of the being who experiences enters into the transaction, which means that the being is not simply a theoretical knower. . . ." But does not *refraction* indicate that the person alters *what is there* and therefore does not *receive* it as it is? Such a theory results in a reality that is unknowable and an "experience" that is unjustifiable.

What is true of the so-called "experience" of a stone is even more obviously true of religious experience. Smith introduced his basic definition of a rich and varied experience for the purpose of defending God and religion from scientism, mechanism, and irreligion. But once again it is impossible to derive any positive religion from "the religious dimension of experience." This leaves unsupported, not so much his denial that Christianity is final and exhaustive (p. 74), as his assertion that Buddhism and Hinduism contain true revelations from God. One would like to see a detailed, step-by-step account of how experience justifies this or that truth in Hinduism. If the alleged truth is definite, even the author admits the gap; but if the truth is vague enough to be found in some form in all three religions, then "God" is the common characteristic of Jehovah, Shiva, and Nirvana; and this is nothing at all. These considerations ruin some twenty pages of non-chalcedonian Christology, as well as the assumptions underlying a discussion of the book of Job.

So far as the present writer can see, the best the author does with this situation is to appeal to a "living reason" that depends on "convincing" conversation, which by the canons of logic is fallacious (chapter IV). Such fallacious "living reason" can "develop the content of experience" (p. 121) in any direction one wishes. Christianity, liberal or orthodox, Buddhism, and Hinduism follow equally well.

Popular Religion

Nowhere in this book has religion been defined. At the beginning it was noted merely that religion had something to do with God. This led to discussions most people would call philosophical and would hardly recognize as religious at all. Yet they must admit that knowledge has to be possible, if one wishes to defend theological statements. There followed therefore the historic proofs of the existence of God and an analysis of the epistemology on which they were based. The last author quoted, after he had finished his epistemological remarks, came somewhat closer to popular interests in religion. Not to leave these interests with so slight a mention, C.F. Potter (*Creative Personality*, Funk and Wagnalls, 1950) will serve as a second example. Since it is usually the case that the more popular a writer is, the less profound and analytic, one must not expect logical perfection in this material. So obvious are its faults that an account written for mature scholars would simply report in outline what Dr. Potter says; but it may not be amiss to point out to students some points that need to be pointed out. These will appear as footnotes.

Since the arts, sex, narcotics, and money are insufficient to remove the inevitable frustrations of life, says Dr. Potter, man turns to religion, and especially to the belief in immortality. But science has made the old doctrines of immortality untenable. Therefore some people redefine immortality to mean the impossibility of annihilating matter, or the begetting of future generations, or the permanence of social institutions, or the continuance of one's influence after death. These are not satisfactory. But now science can give us something better: Evolution will produce the creative personality.*

This bridge between the old religion of revelation and the new religion of science, between theism and humanism, is that kind of religious experience usually known, rather unsatisfactorily, as mysticism, or, better, as cosmic-consciousness, which is achieved when the individual is both intuitively and rationally aware of the universe and his intimate relation to it (p. 7).

Long ago, matter spontaneously became alive. Now a saltation, a jump ahead is imminent.† Man's great characteristic is self-consciousness; but the new species will have cosmic-consciousness. The individuals of this species will be conscious of the cosmos. This new species has already occurred but was unable to reproduce. Moses, Zoroaster, Jesus, and Paul had visions of a great light. Of course the reports these mystics gave of their experience need not be believed; the important thing is the feeling of peace that follows their mystic trance.‡ These

---

* What scientific method is there for predicting the future course of evolution? If one could know that a new species is to emerge a thousand or a million years from now, would that make our present life more worthwhile, less frustrated, and more satisfying than old-fashioned personal immortality? If some depersonalized scientist answers in the affirmative, would the united mine workers, the migrants, and the office clerks find solace in this new religion?

† A million years is too long to wait. The new species is imminent. Next week perhaps. And does this give us peace and tranquility? Was it good news to the animals when man evolved? Were they safer? Did they see their frustrations resolved in this new species? And what scientific information is there that next week's new species will help rather than harm us?

‡ If we cannot believe the reports given by ancient mystics, how can we know that they experienced a feeling of peace, or that they were mystics at all?

men were exceptions, but now, at the latest next week, science instead of religion will be able to make this the normal experience of everyone. The scientific method of producing cosmic-consciousness will be better than that of religion, for religion needed to use trances and science does not.

"The most important thing in all the universe . . . is human personality. . . . Man is the chief product of evolution. Since he is conscious and able to think and plan and act creatively . . . evolution must go on through him" (p. 113).*

The difference that separates ordinary men from the higher variety, like Jesus and Buddha, is that these had a mystic experience. All mystic experience is essentially identical in pattern. It has nine characteristics.† By this experience all mystics attain a cosmic-consciousness. This is not astronomy or physics. It is attained by emotion or intuition. Nevertheless mysticism is supported by the scientific fact that the smallest inert particles vibrate with motion and that "our life . . . is merely a higher form of motion" (p. 152).‡

---

* Is the cosmic-consciousness an evolutionary product, a new species, or simply a man improved by science? If it is an evolutionary "saltation," and is therefore no longer man, then human personality is not, or at least will not be the most important thing in all the universe or the chief product of evolution. Further, the inference that evolution must go on through man because he is a thinking being is invalid. The more complicated species, instead of being the fittest for survival, are most likely to become extinct. Algae have survived longer than the ivory-billed woodpecker, and worms have outlasted dinosaurs. Why should not man disappear in a sulphur dioxide fog or a nuclear holocaust? And again, on what evolutionary or natural principle can one species be judged to be the most important thing in all the universe? Xenophanes and Rupert Brooke tried to ridicule theism because of its anthropomorphic conceit. But evolutionary conceit is worse because it cannot claim the defense that man was created in the image of God.

† Presumably Plotinus was a mystic. He is frequently cited as an outstanding example. But he had few of these nine characteristics, nor did he recover from his trances with the tremendous driving power that Potter says inevitably follows (pp. 138-147).

‡ So, as we contemplate our death, burial, and decay, we can avoid frustration by knowing that our material particles will forever continue to vibrate with motion!

There are several *"Varieties of Immortality"* (chapter viii), or, at least several varieties of belief in immortality, for it is not clear whether Potter accepts all of the earlier items in the list. Presumably he accepts the first as well as the last. The mystics, he says, are uniformly conscious that they experience immortality *now,* not in the future. Hence man in general is becoming conscious of his immortality. Men yearn for immortality, for there is an evolutionary urge to do so. It is not so much a yearning for personal survival (p. 170), for ideas of heaven are revolting. Immortality must be understood otherwise, as something deeper, a desire to extend personality beyond its present limits.

A second form is the belief in the indestructibility of matter. A third form relies on the continuance of the germ plasm that lives on in our descendants. This third theory is defective because some people have no descendants. There is also the immortality of influence and that of social institutions.

A frequently held view is the immortality of personality (p. 173). It is not likely that personality perishes. Personality is the goal of evolution, and if chemicals do not perish, then the higher forms of matter will not perish: The highest product will not perish if the lowest does not. This argument has great weight with many people.*

Many scientists today speak of religion. Einstein really understood religion and attained the cosmic-consciousness. Therefore he dared "to oppose war because it is against this

---

* The arguments, or, better, the hope that complicated forms of matter will not perish can hardly have weight with many people if they but think. The fallacy of the argument is glaring. Not only is it a logical fallacy, but the ad hominem reply to Potter is that higher forms have already perished. As for the substantial question of immortality, it can hardly be true that mystics are conscious they have immortality now and not in the future. They may indeed be unconscious that they will continue in personal existence after death; but how can they know they will not so survive? They might commit suicide to find out. In this case they could find out that they were wrong, but they would never find out that they were right. This gives Dr. Potter one consolation: If he believes that heaven is repulsive or revolting, he can be sure of not getting there.

cosmic religious sense." But "several of them [scientists]. . . are guilty of the scientific sin of using certain religious terms in a sense far different from the meaning understood by the average person" (p. 188). The word *God* is one of the vaguest words. Yet an impersonal god cannot be a God at all. God must be good, and goodness exists only in persons. At the same time, a supernatural God is unscientific. One should ask, Is cosmic energy personal? It is, at least in man. In man's cosmic-consciousness the universe is conscious of itself. Man henceforth can direct evolution. Thus in the future evolution, or, better, advolution, will subordinate personal liberty to social progress. We need a government that will plan our biological, social, economic, and cultural lives.*

Conclusion

Empirical religion, as this chapter has shown, runs the gamut from Thomas' scholastic cosmological argument,

---

* Einstein and Potter may oppose war, and may have preferred a victory by Hitler rather than United States intervention, but they could hardly base their pacifism on an evolutionary nature red in tooth and claw. Evolution is certainly a militaristic theory. And if cosmic-consciousness is not militaristic, how does one show that it demands a totalitarian government to control our biological and cultural lives? Heaven may be revolting; but there can be no revolt against Big Brother. Finally, if it is a scientific sin to use religious terms in a sense far different from their historical and linguistic meanings, who is more guilty than Potter himself? From the time of Job, not to mention Plato, even Plato, immortality was always conceived as personal. There may have been a few guilty scientists or philosophers along the way, but whatever the language was, Latin, French, German, or English, the word immortality always referred to personal survival. Immortality now and not later was, and is, bad language as well as bad theology. So too the word *God.* Potter is quite correct to note the linguistic solecism in speaking of an impersonal God. But when the only cosmic-consciousness he can find, the only case of cosmic energy in personal form, is man, does not this reduction of God to man violate the Queen's English and American dialects as much as any of the guilty scientists Potter condemns? Admittedly this is an ad hominem objection; but the logical gaps and fallacies from beginning to end are not.

through Kant's critical *Religion Within The Limits of Mere Reason,* all the way on to hunches and even trances. The former made serious efforts at logic and scholarship. Potter, for all his encomiums on science, was the least scientific and most wildly fallacious of all. Other popular writers may not be quite so bad as he, but they all leave wide gaps between their basic experience and their propositional conclusions.

It is not surprising that religious experience *sui generis,* aesthetic response, hunches and trances should be useless and miserable, but the chapter has also shown the futility of sensation. No one can make any progress until this conclusion is admitted. It is an unpopular conclusion. Physicists who have learned something of operationalism have begun to see that laboratory experimentation gives no knowledge of how nature moves. Religious authors and the general public still cling tenaciously to sensation. But if they do not meet the skeptical arguments in detail, if they refuse to examine them—mirages, hallucinations, circumstantial variations, and even Descartes' demon—if they refuse to face their opponents squarely, skepticism must be adjudged the victor.

IV

IRRATIONALISM

The title of this book is *Three Types of Religious Philosophy.* This chapter treats of a fourth type. Unfortunately, it is not a type of religious philosophy at all. It is not a philosophy; and the reason is that it is not a method. Nevertheless it follows rather naturally from the last chapter. One who has become disillusioned with empirical methodology, both for its secularistic humanism and its skeptical nihilism, might ask, Why not renounce logic and method and cling desperately to irrational experience? Why should experience have to be logical?

Hume to Hegel

In modern history, however, irrationalism did not immediately follow upon empiricism. Rather it began as a reaction against Hegel's rationalism. The story can be condensed, suffering the usual deficiencies of abbreviation.

Hume had reduced empiricism to skepticism. Kant tried to rescue a role for sensation by positing forms of the mind, innate or apriori, by which sense data could be organized. Knowledge was a compound of these two factors. Sensation by itself is chaotic; apriori forms by themselves are empty; neither factor alone gives knowledge. The forms of space and time organize sensation, and twelve apriori categories organize thought. But, and this is the difficulty, if sensory data can be known only as organized, one cannot know what is the nature of things-in-themselves before they have been altered by the forms of the mind. Thus Kant's philosophy faced the paradox of confidently asserting the existence of something unknowable. The trouble lies in the impossibility of accounting for the data, the given, *das Gegebenes.*

Although God was one of the unknowable objects, Kant allowed man to have a certain kind of faith based on morality. Schleiermacher developed this hint by basing religion on a non-rational religious feeling and by obtaining theological propositions through analysis of this feeling. This line of procedure by-passed Hegel and became the basis of modernism. From modernism came humanism. Now in the twentieth century humanism has no use for apriori Kantian forms and has relapsed into purely empirical methods. Since these have been sufficiently discussed, it is proper to continue with the main philosophical development in the person of Hegel.

Hegel felt keenly the difficulty of asserting an unknowable object. It is impossible, he argued, to set a limit to knowledge. If one selects X as a limit of the ocean, one must know that beyond that limit there is something other than the ocean; and to know that land is other than the ocean is to have some knowledge of land. Similarly, to know that there is a limit to knowledge *i.e.,* to know that there is an Unknowable (and not something merely unknown as yet) requires some knowledge of the Unknowable and is therefore a self-contradictory concept. Now, Kant had invented the Unknowable *Ding an sich* to account for what is given in experience. Since this account is now known to be impossible, it follows that the source of sensation, the given, must be located in the mind, not in something external. Thus Hegel reestablished rationalism. He was so successful that he gave the ponderous appearance of claiming omniscience with all problems completely solved. Hegel was not guilty of quite all the charges brought against him. He was perhaps somewhat pompous. Since too the problems were indeed difficult, and the solutions over-optimistic, it is natural that a reaction occurred.

Rationalism came to be looked on as impossible and therefore Irrationalism was accepted as the religious "non-solution" of all of life's troubles. So said Soren Kierkegaard.

Soren Kierkegaard and the Individual

In addition to a little pomposity and a semblance of omniscience, there was a definite point at which the anti-Hegelian reaction (Feuerbach and Marx as well as Kierkegaard) took aim. It was the existence of the individual. When Hegel attempted to deduce Kant's inexplicable given, the data of sensation, he analyzed one concept after another, arranging them in a cohesive System—a word his opponents spelled with a capital S in derision. Such a system of concepts is a system of universals. Admittedly the concepts of Being, Quality, Cause, etc., are universals; but so also are the concepts of Life, Motion, Soul, and Reason, all of which are in Hegel's list of some two hundred categories. But, objected his opponents, there is no motion in the concept of Motion; my pen, with which the obscure Herr Krug challenged the great professor, cannot be deduced from the concept of Thing; and, more important, I myself cannot be found in Life or Reason. Individuals, both things and persons, do not occur in the System. Hegel could not explain *himself.* Maybe the System had a place for The Philosopher, but Hegel himself, Descartes and Aristotle were absent.

Many people regard this circumstance as fatal to rationalism. Kierkegaard had a further reason for reacting against empty universals. He was a Christian; at least he talked as he thought Christians ought to talk; and since Christianity offers eternal salvation to human individuals, individuals are important in the extreme. Whether the Philosopher succeeds or fails in properly arranging the concepts of Being and Life is a trivial matter; but whether I myself, just this one individual person, me, attains heaven is a matter of eternal life or eternal death.

Historical Events

There are also other individuals that strike Kierkegaard's attention, though with a different result: *viz.*, individual historical events. Now, if Herr Krug's pen was sufficiently pointed to puncture Hegel's pomposity, one would think that existentialism, concerned as it is for individual existences, would show some interest in individual events. Is not Napoleon more important to an historian than a pen? And must not a Christian take an interest in Jesus of Nazareth? Through the centuries Christianity has taught that Jesus Christ was crucified under Pontius Pilate and on the third day rose from the dead. These are dated, historical, individual events. But, strangely, Kierkegaard is completely uninterested. He asks, in italics, "Is an historical point of departure possible for an eternal consciousness;* how can such a point of departure have any other than a mere historical interest; is it possible to base an eternal happiness upon historical knowledge?" (on the title page of the *Philosophical Fragments* and repeated on p. 18 of the *Concluding Unscientific Postscript*, tr. by Swenson and Lowrie). Traditional Apologetics and Theological Prolegomena used these events to prove the truth of Christianity or used various historical evidences to prove the truth of these events. But Kierkegaard will "not raise the question of the truth of Christianity," nor is he interested in "the systematic zeal of the personally indifferent individual to arrange the truths of Christianity in paragraphs." What Kierkegaard will discuss is "the concern of the infinitely interested individual for his own relationship to such a doctrine" (*Concluding Unscientific Postscript*, pp. 18-19).

One reason for ignoring the truth of Christianity is the

---

* Since orthodox Christianity denies that human consciousness is eternal (for it had a beginning in time and its psychological moments are temporal), it would appear that some of S.K.'s arguments are irrelevant.

impossibility of discovering what happened in history. History is an empirical study and empiricism makes knowledge impossible. Did Christ die and rise? Was there ever a preacher in Palestine named Jesus? Can we discover anything he ever said or did? Historical investigation to determine these facts requires a study of documents. Are the documents genuine or not? Did Matthew copy Mark's mistakes? Was John written after A.D. 150? How shall opposing evidences be judged? Judged they must be: They must be balanced, the ones against the others. Newly discovered evidence changes the balance. Historical study therefore results in a series of approximations, and approximation leads to despair, for no one ever gets to heaven by approximations.*

Scholarship never ends. Therefore the scholar can never decide. One can admire Ciceronian scholarship because it aims at nothing more than accuracy about Cicero. Here approximation is not embarrassing. But Biblical scholarship, used to establish the truth of historical events, claims to give eternal life. This, unlike Cicero, is a matter of infinite passion, and for infinite passion and eternal life a single iota is of infinite importance.†

Suppose historical research proved the Bible true. Would this help anyone who did not have faith? No, for faith is not the result of scholarly inquiry. It does not bring a person one step closer to faith. Would such proof of the Biblical events help the person who already has faith? No, for several reasons. First, since he has faith, nothing further is needed. Second, research may actually harm him because objectivity tends to dissipate infinite passion. Then third, according to this supposition the

---

* Though Kierkegaard had few friends during his lifetime, his problem was taken up by Martin Kähler toward the end of the century, and his outlook contributed greatly, one might say, controlled the development of dialectical theology through Barth, Bultmann, et al.

† With all this distaste for doctrine, was Kierkegaard thinking of *homo-ousia* and *homoi-ousia?*

person would know that the Bible is true; he would have knowledge, and therefore he would have lost his faith. Faith requires passion and certainty excludes passion. Faith does not need theology or scholarship for the same reason that a girl in love does not need to have a respectable boy friend.*

At the start one might have thought that Kierkegaard would be interested in history simply because Hegel was not. If there is no motion in the concept of Motion, and no Hegel in the concept of Man, does it not follow that the Absolute System has no place for history? But by Kierkegaard's analysis Hegel has too much history. Hegel identifies the truth with the unfolding of the Absolute in history. This is fatal. In a long footnote *(Concluding Unscientific Postscript,* p. 34) Kierkegaard ridicules Hegel. The latter's Absolute System is not unchanging Truth; it is chaotic skepticism. Since for Hegel truth is the continuing world process, each stage is valid; the opinions of every age are true—at the moment. But since history still continues no thinker or culture has arrived at the final truth. What is true today will be false tomorrow. In Hegel everything is as relative as it was in Protagoras. The ridicule of this footnote does not depend on Kierkegaard's rejection of relativism. For him too, in the footnote on the following page:

> The infinite reflection in which alone the concern of the subject for his eternal happiness can realize itself has in general one distinguishing mark—the omnipresence of the dialectical. . . . Even the most fixed of things, an infinite negative resolve, the infinite form for God's presence in the individual, at once

---

* An interesting analogy, is it not? It carries the unintended suggestion that S.K. has misunderstood what Christianity is. Historical scholarship, if indeed it proved the Bible true, would, despite S.K.'s assertion, be of help. It would not generate faith, to be sure, but it would provide the object of faith. In the case of the man who already has faith, this scholarship would strengthen or mature his faith, and hence would not be useless. Nor does the New Testament teach that knowledge is incompatible with faith. Compare II Peter 1:3; 3:18 *et passim.* However, the present purpose is to examine S.K.'s own position, regardless of whether or not he misrepresents Christianity.

becomes dialectical. As soon as I take the dialectical away, I become superstitious. . . . But it is far more comfortable to be objective and superstitious, and boastful about it, proclaiming thoughtlessness as wisdom.

Thus Kierkegaard is as dialectical, as relativistic, and as skeptical as he believes Hegel is. The ridicule consists in this: Hegel thought he was objective; Kierkegaard openly accepts irrationalism.

The morbid Dane illustrates the dialectical difficulties—the evaporation of one truth into another—both as they occur in Romanism with its ultimate appeal to the Church and in Protestantism with its ultimate appeal to the Bible. The latter was as comical as Don Quixote. Its passion was good, but its object was wrong. The first dialectical difficulty with the Bible is that it is an historical document, and the resulting troubles have already been mentioned. To avoid them Romanism appeals to the Church. The Church is not an historical document: It is a present reality that needs no proof. Yet the Romanists claim that the present Church is the apostolic Church. Therefore questions of history are not avoided. Historical proof is needed, and the approximation process begins over again. It would be necessary to prove historically the primitive and apostolic character of the Council of Trent and of the Church as a whole "in every moment through eighteen centuries (where criticism will stumble on difficulties that the Bible theory never knew)." A person who bases his eternal happiness on the Church is as comic as Don Quixote; not because of his passion—that is good, but because "the objectivity-of-the-Church theory is incommensurable with his interest" *(Concluding Unscientific Postscript,* p. 42).

Here let us pause to catch our breath. The argument on historical research is acutely embarrassing to that type of (Lutheran) Apologetics and Prolegomena that tries to prove various Christian theses by archaeology or historical investigation. It is impossible by historical methods to prove beyond all doubt that Jesus was crucified. Even if the crucifixion be probable (though what probability means is not easily explained), empirical history could never prove that his death was a propitiatory sacrifice. And without this latter belief the former cannot save. But such difficulties as these do not embarrass any Christian who rejects empirical methodology. The impossibilities that attach to sensation and memory in all instances naturally attach also in the case of history. Besides, history has further difficulties of its own.* Kierkegaard therefore seems to be justified in repudiating empirical, historical methodology; though he may be quite mistaken in thinking that this eliminates historical events from religion.

Skepticism

One must not minimize or extenuate Kierkegaard's skepticism. He makes the point quite clear.

> The positive in the sphere of thought comes under the head of certainty in sense-perception, in historical knowledge, and in speculative results. But all this positiveness is sheer falsity. The certainty afforded by sense-perception is a deception, as one may learn from a study of the Greek skeptics,† and from the entire treatment of this subject in the writings of modern idealism, which is very instructive. The positiveness of historical knowledge is illusory, since it is approximation-knowledge; the speculative result is a delusion *(Concluding Unscientific Postscript*, p. 75).

---

* Compare Clark, *Historiography: Secular and Religious* (Nutley, New Jersey: Presbyterian and Reformed Publishing Company, 1972).

† This reference to the Greek skeptics confirms the fact, otherwise clear in the context, that Kierkegaard is not merely reporting Hegel's strictures on sensation at the beginning of the *Phenomenology.* The Greek skeptics and modern idealism—a phrase that at least includes Berkeley and Hume—convince him of skepticism.

Irrationalism

Reason is as illusory as sensation. Scattered through his writings are various attacks on reason or rationality. For example, reason cannot begin. It entails an infinite regress. If everything must be reasoned out, there can be no unreasoned first premise. Hence reason cannot begin. This line of argument may or may not have some force against Euclid or Spinoza. But the objection sounds much more formidable when directed against Hegel.

> The System so it is said, begins with the immediate . . . hence without any presuppositions, and hence absolutely; the beginning of the System is an absolute beginning. But . . . how does the system begin with the immediate? . . . Does it begin with it immediately? The answer to this question must be an unconditional negative. If the System is presumed to come after existence . . . then the System is of course *ex post facto,* and so does not begin immediately with the immediacy with which existence began; although in another sense it may be said that existence did not begin with the immediate, since the immediate never is as such, but is transcended as soon as it is. The beginning which begins with the immediate *is thus itself reached by means of a process of reflection (Concluding Unscientific Postscript,* pp. 101-102).

Kierkegaard regards this as a fatal objection to Hegelianism, and he takes the opportunity to point up its application to the existing individual. If reflection has no first premise, no conclusion, and can never end, the Professor can never become a human being. No conclusion means, particularly means, no decision. The Professor cannot decide to stop reflecting and go to dinner. In order to act, a human being must stop reasoning. To act is to break through reflection in an arbitrary act of will.

Kierkegaard, however, is not destructive and negative only; he obviously is an advocate of something. This advocacy and this something require attention. In the place of objectivity

Kierkegaard proposes subjectivity, faith, and infinite passion. Now, ordinarily faith means a belief in something, if only in the efficacy of curing warts by drinking vinegar. But the something that Kierkegaard proposes as the object of faith is neither so definite nor so intellectual as a belief in the virtues of vinegar. Faith does not need the Bible; faith does not need theology; knowing that something is true only harms and destroys faith. What then does the neurotic Dane mean by faith? Does the phrase *infinite passion* answer this question? What is infinite passion? Surely Kierkegaard cannot want us to know what faith and passion are because, if we knew, we would have destroyed them. Many pages later in the book its author defines faith as "the objective uncertainty due to the repulsion of the absurd held by the passion of inwardness . . . intensified to the utmost degree" *(Concluding Unscientific Postscript,* p. 540). Something yet needs to be said about absurdity, but, subject to this further explanation, does this definition of faith convey any meaning whatever?

Communication

To an extent, possibly to a large extent, Kierkegaard realized that he had not and could not communicate anything. How can a man, he asks, communicate the conviction that truth is subjectivity and inwardness? Therefore Kierkegaard relies on an indirect communication. Socratic irony, jesting, ridicule may possibly suggest what cannot possibly be said. But is this so, or has Kierkegaard misunderstood Socrates? Socrates used irony as a pedagogical device: It held the attention of those who otherwise would shut their ears in fatuous self-satisfaction. Socrates also used dialectical questioning to draw the truth out of young but serious students. His dialectic, however, was not Hegelian dialectics, in which all is Heraclitean flux. Socrates was sharp in his ridicule of those who could not step into the same thought twice, but were always changing their opinions.

And no matter how ironic or indirect his method was, he did not aim to produce an unintelligent and unintelligible infinite passion. Socrates aimed to produce clearcut definitions "which can be memorized"—a phrase with which Kierkegaard sarcastically castigates intellectualists.

Perhaps, however, insistence on the fact that Kierkegaard has misunderstood Socrates as much as he has misunderstood Christianity is irrelevant. He has his own theory of indirect communication, and it is this that one must examine. Now, supposing that Kierkegaard could, by his indirect method, somehow stimulate an infinite passion in his pupil, he could not know that he had now experienced what Kierkegaard intended. Still, even though neither could know it, just perhaps the infinite passion has been aroused. Then what? What good is it? Does it, as Gospel information claims to do, lead to eternal happiness? What makes Kierkegaard think that it does? Did he ever receive from God the intellectually understood information that information was worthless and passion guaranteed heaven? Surely Kierkegaard's embarrassment here is more Quixotic than Church, Bible, or even Hegel.

Absurdity

Nevertheless Kierkegaard is not altogether opposed to intellectual understanding. He even insists on its necessity. But its role may at first occasion some surprise. The matter is connected with the mention of absurdity in his definition of faith. Passionate inwardness holds fast to the absurd in faith. But to hold to the absurd because it is absurd requires clear understanding.

In one place his explanation goes like this.

> Without risk there is no faith, and the greater the risk, the greater the faith. . . .
> When Socrates believed that there was a God, he held fast

to the objective uncertainty with the whole passion of his
inwardness, and it is precisely in this contradiction and in this
risk, that faith is rooted. Now it is otherwise. Instead of the
objective uncertainty, there is here a certainty, namely, that
objectively it is absurd; and this absurdity, held fast in the passion
of inwardness, is faith. The Socratic ignorance is like a witty jest
in comparison with the earnestness of facing the absurd. . . .

What now is the absurd? The absurd is—that the eternal
truth has come into being in time, that God has come into being,
has been born, has grown up, and so forth . . . *(Concluding
Unscientific Postscript,* p. 188).

Kierkegaard does not mean that the Incarnation and
whatever other Christian doctrines he may have in mind are
surprising or psychologically incredible to heathen peasants
and German philosophers. It is not as if the common sense of
the sinful human race never expected an atonement and
resurrection. This is not what Kierkegaard means by paradox
and absurdity. He means precisely that the doctrines are
self-contradictory, therefore meaningless, therefore absurd.
This is why a certain amount of intellectual ability and activity
must accompany faith. "He [a Christian] may very well have
understanding (indeed he must have it in order to believe
against understanding)" *(ibid.,* p. 503).

This is a point to be noticed. Orthodox or traditional
theologians have often said that the truths of revelation are not
against reason but above reason. For Kierkegaard the *above*
has no particular meaning, and faith is strictly *against* reason.
This is why understanding and reason are essential.

Every man . . . can qualitatively . . . distinguish . . . between what he understands and what he does not understand.
. . . When he stakes his life on the absurd, he makes the motion in
virtue of the absurd; and he is essentially deceived in case the
absurd he has chosen can be proved to be not the absurd. [To act
in ignorance is not to act *against* reason; acting *against* reason

requires a clear-cut understanding that two propositions are contradictories and a voluntary belief in both.] So . . . a Christian . . . may very well have understanding (indeed he must have it in order to believe against understanding) *(ibid.,* pp. 495-496, 503).

Kierkegaard mentions many examples of absurd Christian doctrines. His chief examples, perhaps in a sense all his examples, depend on the impossibility of a mixture of time and eternity. God is eternal; therefore it is logically impossible for God to appear or act in time. Though one might not think of it at first, not only the Incarnation, but forgiveness of sin also is impossible for the same reason. Forgiveness involves a relationship between eternal truth and an existing individual. It purports to be an eternal decision in time with retroactive power to annul the past. If, however, forgiveness is not a paradox, it cannot be believed. And the believer must believe it. "The individual existing human being must feel himself a sinner . . . with all the strength of his mind . . . he must try to understand the forgiveness of sins. . . . Thus the simple man will doubtless say, '. . . the more vividly I believe it, the less am I able to understand it' " *(ibid.,* 201-204).

Faith

This line of procedure might seem to help the critic to understand what Kierkegaard meant by faith. To ordinary people faith is belief that something is so, like vinegar cures warts. Now the critic discovers that Kierkegaard's faith begins by understanding that two propositions, *e.g.,* God is eternal and God became man, are contradictories. They cannot in any way be harmonized. Faith now has an object, two objects: It believes both contradictories. The Christian believes that God became man and he believes with equal fervor that God could not possibly have become man *(ibid.,* p. 513).

Rather obviously Kierkegaard is not the spokesman for Christianity. Who in the whole history of the church ever believed these two contradictories? Where in the Bible are they asserted? One may, from an atheistic standpoint, condemn Christians for being stupid enough to believe in God; or from a mildly religious standpoint one may call them superstitious for believing the impossible; but who with a straight face can characterize the Christian movement as a belief in contradictories? Christians believe God became incarnate; they emphatically do not believe that he could not become incarnate. What Kierkegaard means by faith is totally at variance with the Christian meaning of faith.

The reason Christians do not believe contradictories is that no one can. A non-christian critic of Kierkegaard will soon discover that he, the critic, is rational and not insane. And unless one is insane, it is impossible by any act of will to believe both of two contradictories, knowing them to be contradictories. True enough, one may hold opposing opinions without knowing it; but when another points out the inconsistency, the victim will try to harmonize the two and argue that they do not conflict, or he will cease to believe one or both. Yet Kierkegaard supposes it possible to understand clearly that *vinegar cures warts* and *vinegar does not cure warts* are two contradictories, and with this clear understanding decide to believe both.

Repudiation of Logic

This matter of the repudiation of the laws of logic calls for a little additional emphasis. Although Kierkegaard has a flair for literary style, waxes rhetorical at times, and pillories his opponents with sarcasm, satire, and scorn, his frequent references to contradictories must be taken at literal face value. To make it clear that the absurd is not just something queer and unfamiliar to popular opinion, he very soberly and earnestly defines it as contradictory.

In so far as the absurd comprehends within itself the factor of becoming, one way of approximation will be that which confuses the absurd fact of such a becoming (which is the object of faith) with a simple historical fact, and hence seeks historical certainty for that which is absurd, because it involves the contradiction that something which can become historical only in direct opposition to all human reason, has become historical. It is this contradiction which constitutes the absurd, and which can only be believed (*ibid.,* 189-190).

Once this explicit rejection of the fundamental law of logic is seen, none of the passages on the *absolute paradox* can be misunderstood. For Kierkegaard a paradox is not something that at first seems puzzling or even impossible to common sense, but which can clearly be explained. This is the meaning of the word in ordinary language. For example, a student of elementary physics is puzzled when told that the weight of water in one container exerts a pressure of x pounds on its bottom, but that half the weight in another container exerts the same pressure or even 2x pounds. The physics professor can easily explain it. College students regularly come up against similar paradoxes in other classes. They are dumbfounded to learn that there are just as many prime numbers as there are numbers. Does this not mean that the part is equal to the whole? And is that not impossible? Others supposedly more advanced than college students find it incredible that a day (the rotation of the earth), a month (the revolution of the moon), and a year (the revolution of the earth around the sun), if all three at any time began simultaneously the same split second, could never again through all eternity begin at the same instant. For they are incommensurable velocities. These are paradoxes as the word is used in ordinary language. But Kierkegaard alters linguistic usage and speaks of paradox as inexplicable (compare *ibid.,* pp. 195-198, 513-514).

The Absolute Paradox therefore is the absolute contradiction. Kierkegaard, far from shrinking back at the thought of denying the laws of logic and becoming irrational, glories in it. The point is important, not only for a correct understanding of Kierkegaard, but also for a correct understanding of Karl Barth and the type of religion he has popularized since World War I.

Barth, Brunner, *et al.*

Before the concluding paragraphs on Soren Kierkegaard, it is useful to refer to his influence in the twentieth century. Although theologians paid him scant attention during his life time, Karl Barth, at the end of World War I, with what was then called the theology of crisis, convinced Europe of the beauty of the Great Dane. Just before World War II Emil Brunner brought the viewpoint to America where it flourished for two decades in the era's intellectual confusion and moral instability. Though it has now lost some of its popularity, there are still hundreds or even thousands of seminary students, professors, and pastors who have sacrificed their intellect and espoused the religion of irrationalism.

In Barth's early writings he made great use of paradoxes. Later in his *Church Dogmatics* he reduced their extent, without eliminating them completely and obscured, but did not deny, his basic irrationalism. The matter comes up as Barth tries to show that theology is not a science (though *Wissenschaft* does not have the positivistic overtones that *Science* has). Barth lists six criteria of science. His irrationalism appears most plainly in his discussion of the first criterion, with some supporting evidence in the second and sixth.

The first criterion is freedom from self-contradiction. Now, any rational person, if charged with condoning contradictions, would clearly and emphatically deny the charge. There would be no hesitation about it. But Barth begins by asserting that theology must restrict the law of contradiction to a very limited interpretation. Note carefully what he says, for the sentence is a bit awkward. "The very minimum postulate of freedom from contradiction is acceptable by theology only upon the very limited interpretation, by the scientific theorist upon the scarcely tolerable one, that theology will not assert an irremovability in principle of the 'contradictions' it is bound to make good" *(Church Dogmatics,* I, 1, p. 8). This somewhat awkward sentence, first of all, admits the law of contradiction, if at all, only in a very minimum of application. Its full logical extent is ruled out immediately. In the second place, the sentence does not really say that even a restricted use of the law is permissible, for it does not assert that contradictions can be removed. It merely asserts that it cannot be asserted that they cannot be removed. But if perchance a contradiction can be removed, then, as the immediately following sentence says, "The propositions in which it asserts their removal will be propositions concerning the free action of God, and so not propositions that 'remove' the contradictions 'from the world.' " It is hard to see what Barth means here. Someone might wish to defend him by supposing that although theological propositions may seem to us to be contradictories, they are not contradictories in God's mind. Unfortunately, the passage does not assert that God's mind is free from contradiction. Nor, even if it were, does Barth explain how a sane man can possibly believe what he thinks is contradictory.

One thing is clear, however. In his various writings Barth made use of Kierkegaard's Paradox, Eternity versus Time, Infinite Qualitative Difference, and Totally Other. Now, when Barth shows so much dependence on Kierkegaard, one would normally suppose that he remains basically irrationalistic, unless he clearly and emphatically rejects the irrationalism of these terms. But by ambiguous or indefinite language he avoids both outright assertion and outright denial of contradiction.

The general tendency is toward irrationalism. Consider his discussion of the sixth criterion of science, which is, all propositions are capable of being broken up into axioms and theorems and are susceptible of proof on this basis. Now, the student of Barth notes with interest that his volume on *Anselm: Fides Quarens Intellectum* seems to accept and apply this criterion. Yet his *Church Dogmatics* rejects it utterly. Theology can never be made systematic: "God's Word is not a thing to be described, nor is it a concept to be defined. It is neither a content nor an idea . . . [nor] a fixed total of revealed propositions" (I, 1, pp. 155-56). Theology "cannot regard itself as a member of an ordered cosmos, but only as a stop-gap in an unordered one" (*ibid.*, p. 9). In view of the Biblical teaching that God is omniscient, that he exercises providential care, and has seen the end from the beginning, no one can regard Barth's unordered cosmos as a Christian conception; but its irrationalism cannot be mistaken. Yet sometimes his procedure, not only in *Anselm* but even in *Church Dogmatics*, seems to utilize axioms and systematization. Once again, however, when he answers Strauss, the irrationalism recurs. Strauss had argued against making the testimony of the Spirit and the authority of Scripture the basis of all theology by asking, "Who can now attest the divinity of this witness?" This he called "the 'Achilles heel' of the Protestant system." Barth seemingly approves of the question, but replies, "What Strauss failed to see is that there is no Protestant system" (*Church Dogmatics*, I, 2, p. 537).

Thus Barth may be described as an irrationalist who wishes to obscure the fact somewhat. Other contemporary theologians are more forthright in their irrationalism. Reinhold Niebuhr explicitly makes use of Kierkegaard's absurdity: "There is no escape from the rational absurdity of the real self, because it is at once in time and beyond time. It is spatial and yet non spatial. . . . Yet this double fact, which outrages the sense of rational coherence, is a fact of daily experience" (*The Self and the Dramas of History*, p. 24). Now, the fact that the self may be spatial in one sense and non-spatial in a different relationship hardly outrages rational coherence; whether the self is both temporal and eternal may be questioned, but at any rate this view does not represent Christianity, for orthodox theology teaches that man, because he was created, is and always will remain temporal. But the quotation shows clearly enough the irrationality of Niebuhr's religion. However, Emil Brunner is perhaps even more forthright than Niebuhr.

Brunner is so obviously and so vigorously irrational that only a point or two need be mentioned.* He holds that God can speak his word to a man even in false propositions. He holds that the Bible is consistently inconsistent. Theology is not concerned with intelligible, rational truth *(einsichtige Vernunfts-wahrheit)*. Further, God and the medium of conceptuality *(Begrifflichkeit)* are mutually exclusive. The contradictions in the Bible are evidences of God's condescension to us. No one can be sure which of the several "systems" in the Bible is the "echo" of the divine Word because there is no unambiguous criterion by which to distinguish them. Finally, with obvious points of dependence on Kierkegaard, Brunner makes full use of Paradox.

Although the present writer is reasonably confident that he has correctly stated the position of these theologians, even in details, historical accuracy is not the main point. The main point is the irrationality of irrationalism. Hence the concluding subsection returns to Kierkegaard.

Conclusion

Irrationalism makes it useless to ask what the object of faith is. Faith really has no object, and Kierkegaard really has no faith. The case of Pascal is an interesting comparison because Kierkegaard's disciples try to enhance his reputation with the reflection of the French philosopher's lustre. In their irrationalism these disciples stress decisions in opposition to conclusions, they speak of a wager (as Brunner in particular

---

* For a full and keen discussion, see Paul King Jewett, *Emil Brunner's Concept of Revelation* (London: James Clarke & Co. Ltd., 1954).

does), and for other reasons claim Pascal as a kindred spirit. The difference, however, is enormous.

Pascal's wager was a mathematical calculation of odds, such as gamblers use. If you win two cents for tossing a head and lose only one cent for tossing a tail, you should by all means gamble. It is hardly a gamble at all, for you are sure to win in the long run. Since there are just two possibilities, you will win half the time and lose half the time. But since, when you win, you win twice as much—well, it is pretty obvious, is it not?

Now, Pascal's wager was equally mathematical, but the odds were infinitely better. Either there is a God or there is not: just like heads and tails. But instead of winning two cents and losing one cent, if you bet on God and win you win infinitely; while if you lose you lose nothing. Conversely, if you bet against God and win, you win nothing; but if you lose, you lose eternal life. In his wager Pascal offers objective mathematical chance. The odds can be calculated. There is nothing irrational. The object of faith is also definite, God. In particular, Pascal does not ask us to believe two contradictory propositions at the same time. Pascal and Kierkegaard are poles apart.

In addition to this illustration, Kierkegaard's own statements clearly make faith impossible. That faith has no object and therefore that there is no faith agrees with the main tenor of Kierkegaard's predilections. In spite of his frequent references to and encomiums of faith, actually Kierkegaard is not interested in faith or belief at all. His recommendation is infinite passion, and this is neither above reason, nor logically against reason, for no propositions at all are in view; it is simply below, far below reason. Further evidence that Kierkegaard had no place for faith in his thought comes in a well-known illustration of a frequently repeated point. In several places Kierkegaard stresses the "how" as opposed to the "what." "The thing of being a Christian," he says, "is not determined by the *what* of Christianity, but by the *how* of the Christian." Kierkegaard does not mean, as a naive believer might suppose, that being a

Christian requires not only the Biblical doctrines printed on the page, but also an individual's acceptance of, assent to, or belief in those doctrines. He continues, "This *how* can only correspond with one thing, the absolute paradox. There is therefore no vague talk to the effect that being a Christian, is to accept, and to accept, and to accept quite differently, to appropriate, to believe, to appropriate by faith quite differently (all of them purely rhetorical and fictitious definitions)." The subsidiary point in this passage is not well taken. Kierkegaard with his rhetorical flair has added some vague language; but not all of these orthodox phrases or definitions are fictitious and vague. For the simple Christian, what could be clearer than the statement, "If thou shalt confess that Jesus is Lord and believe God raised him from the dead, thou shalt be saved"? But though this subsidiary point is not well taken, Kierkegaard's connection of the *how* with the absolute paradox is unambiguous.

Kierkegaard's well-known illustration of the *how* is as follows.

> If one who lives in the midst of Christianity goes up to the house of God, the house of the true God, with the true conception of God in his knowledge, and prays, but prays in a false spirit; and one who lives in an idolatrous community prays with the entire passion of the infinite, although his eyes rest upon the image of an idol: where is there most truth? The one prays in truth to God though he worships an idol; the other prays falsely to the true God, and hence worships in fact an idol *(Concluding Unscientific Postscript,* pp. 179-180).

The illustration is striking, but like all illustrations misleading. In the first place, a comparison between sincerity and hypocrisy is invidious. Presumably Kierkegaard wants to illustrate the difference between intellectualism and emotionalism. But to picture the intellectualist as hypocritical is dishonest propaganda. In the second place, an illustration cannot add any value to a Hindu's idolatrous worship that the argument has not demonstrated. But the only value mentioned is sincerity, and this value intellectualists have as often as Hindus. If Kierkegaard dishonestly insists on the antithesis between sincerity and hypocrisy, we shall treat him more fairly than he has treated us. His question was, On which side was there the more truth? We reply: on the side of the allegedly hypocritical intellectualist. But we shall treat him more fairly by rephrasing his question: On which side is the greater religious value? The answer is: On neither side, if indeed the intellectualist is insincere. Both sides are valueless. This is not the answer Kierkegaard wanted, but nothing in the illustration necessitates what he wants.

The conclusion is now more than plain. There is no need to complain that Kierkegaard has neglected to define a few terms, that he uses more ridicule than thought, or that his illustrations are beside the point. The fatal flaw is his rejection of logic. When once a man commits himself to contradictions, his language, and therefore his recommendations to other people, become meaningless. He tells us, Don't trust Hegel. But if contradictions are in order, we can trust Hegel and refuse to trust him at the same time. If God became incarnate and could not possibly have become incarnate, could not Hegel's and Kierkegaard's books be equally true and valuable? Then if this sort of truth does not matter—and this sort of nonsense indeed does not—and everything depends on a purely subjective passion, why cannot we direct our passion toward the devil as well as toward God? We can. The *what* is unimportant; only the *how* counts. And what good is the *how?* Will the most passionate belief in vinegar cure warts if there is no vinegar? Will the deceived fiancée achieve marital bliss by marrying her dissolute beau?

If historical information, such as "Christ died," and its intellectual explanation, "for our sins," cannot bring eternal blessedness, why should one think that an infinitely passionate appropriation of nothing could do the trick? Empty nihilism is the meaning of empirical philosophy and empirical religion.

V

DOGMATISM

Dogmatism is in ill repute. If there were any chance of avoiding it, in either rationalism or empiricism, nearly everyone would choose to avoid it. But these two highly respected philosophies are failures. Well, then, would one prefer irrationalism to dogmatism? How would it be to experience an infinite passion, a passion that never ceases (for if it ceased, it would not be infinite), a passion that palpitates and leaves one out of breath from morning till night, and perhaps in one's dreams too? Could even drug addiction be worse?

Suicide

There is a more satisfactory way, perhaps, of escaping dogmatism. Suicide. This seems to be more satisfactory because irrationalism cannot assign a purpose, reason, or justification for living. This was the way out Van Gogh used. When he perceived that his fits of irrationality would continue and get worse, he concluded in his last moments of sanity that such a purposeless life was worse than death. A rational life requires a purpose. Such a purpose must be regarded as a fixed truth. Can anyone justify life and bend all energies toward an end that he knows he will reject tomorrow? The irrationalist and the empiricist with their all-encompassing Heraclitean flux do indeed know that tomorrow they must abandon their most cherished concepts. What futility! That life is worth living, that a rational purpose alone can condemn suicide as immoral, requires that value and that purpose to be fixed principles. They must be definite principles, not vague or amorphous. One would in rational consistency have to state what the good was that made life better. Then would come the choice of methods for pursuing, approximating, or achieving this good. In fact one would need a System. But rationalism and empiricism, no less than irrationalism, are incapable of providing a system to make life worth while. These all prevent even drug addiction from being the good.

Therefore to escape drug addiction, to escape irrationalism, to escape suicide, what else is there but dogmatism? At the least, if one can postpone suicide for five minutes, dogmatism deserves consideration as the only possible alternative to futility.

The God of Dogmatism

It will be objected that this makes dogmatism a *Deus ex machina*. There is indeed a resemblance. An old literary critic in all seriousness laid down a rule that makes one smile: a *Deus ex machina* should never be used unless the author has so tangled up his plot that no other solution is possible. This rule is applicable here because there is no other possibility. However it is not the dogmatist who has tangled up the plot. The plot or problem is itself the tangle. It was not the dogmatist who made sensation chaotic and inferences from it fallacious. These difficulties were first written out by people who were not dogmatists. Hence by the fixed truth of literary criticism a *Deus ex machina* is a rational solution.

Yet dogmatism is not precisely a *Deus ex m*. In the eyes of its opponents it is worse. The literary device is used just once at the end of the play. But in dogmatism God and his revelation are invoked at every step of the way. Is this worse, or is it better? Do not logic, consistency, and System require God's action to be pervasive, rather than restricting it to Act V Scene IX? The God of dogmatism is a sovereign Deity who determines all his creatures and all their actions.

Similarities to Rationalism

One can hardly hope that dyed-in-the-empirical philosophers will give any favorable consideration to dogmatism. Rationalists, however, might; for there are certain similarities. Dogmatism like rationalism posits a first principle. Whether or not Hegel is vulnerable to Kierkegaard's criticism that reason cannot begin, that the System has no presuppositions, that there is an infinite regress, etc., rationalism and dogmatism are not in this respect vulnerable. Aristotle, empiricist that he was, defended logical argument against the accusation of infinite regress. He insisted on first principles of demonstration. True, he made sensory experience prior to demonstration. In this his empiricism must fail. Aristotle's account of how a concept is obtained from sensation or how one comes to recognize a principle as first, lacks all explanatory plausibility.

In the *Posterior Analytics* Aristotle says that from repeated memories of the same time a universal concept is formed. He even tells how it is formed. It is like a rout in battle being stopped by first one man making a stand, and then another, and so on until order has been restored. But no one can follow Aristotle in this. He has not given an explanation; he has only used a figure of speech. Such literary devices mean nothing. They do not enlighten; they obscure. A few lines later Aristotle drops the figure, or half drops it, and the barrenness of his explanation is evident. When one of a number of logically indiscriminable particulars has made a stand, he says, then for the first time there is a universal in the soul, and the process does not stop until we get the ten categories and the first principles of the several sciences (not completely verbatim). But these phrases do not quite avoid the figure of speech, nor do they otherwise explain *how* the particular becomes a universal.

Although Aristotle's empiricism is a failure, if first principles can be had in some other way, demonstration and system escape infinite regress. Rationalism does not produce first principles out of something else: The first principles are innate. And this is not far removed from the dogmatism or fideism that simply posits them as Euclid did.

This is a point to keep in mind. It removes the basis on which dogmatism is adjudged irrational and disreputable. Every philosophy must have its first principles. Even modern empiricism. Mention will be made of two cases in point. First, William James *(Principles of Psychology,* 1890) refuted the view that empirical description could be conducted without prior assumptions. In this he attacked the dominant nineteenth century view. Science in those days was supposed to be final and completely free from the apriori. D.F. Strauss early in the century had applied this principle to history and claimed to have written a *Leben Jesu* without having made any assumptions. It was a most prejudiced book. Even after James' *Psychology* had appeared the phenomenologists of this century held that they could give empirical descriptions unaffected by intellectual construction. They failed to note that the concepts and classifications they had to use as predicates were already results of previous choices. Thus a presuppositionless description is impossible.

The second case in point, however similar it may be, is Logical Positivism. This school held that a sentence is meaningful, as opposed to being nonsense, only if it is verifiable by sensory experience. For a long time the assertion "The other side of the moon has no mountains" could not be actually verified or falsified; but it was meaningful because it was verifiable in principle. A few people have now seen the other side of the moon, and their experience discovers whether the assertion is true or false. Either way it is not nonsense: It has meaning. But what is in principle unverifiable by sensation is strictly nonsense—it is a sentence without meaning. Naturally the aim of this theory was to make metaphysics and theology nonsense.

This logical positivism has now experienced many vicissitudes. Its early formulations implied results that were distasteful to its authors. Neither God nor the Hegelian Absolute could be denied meaning. Reformulations followed; and these too proved unacceptable to the school. But aside from these internal difficulties, Alvin Plantinga* asked, Even if the logical positivists could formulate a principle that would separate sentences into meaningful and meaningless in a manner satisfactory to the positivists, why should anyone accept it? Given this not-yet formulated principle, it would follow that Christian theology is meaningless. The positivistic inference would be valid; but why should one accept its premise?

Beyond this the crushing reply to empirical verificationism is that on its own principle it itself is meaningless. The principle, A sentence is meaningful only if verifiable by sense, can itself never be verified by sense. Thus by its own test logical positivism is nonsense. Attempts to avoid the technical difficulties, Plantinga's unanswerable question, and the final objection have led to alterations so extensive that one may call the original view dead. Other principles have replaced it.

John Wisdom and Ian Ramsey have their principles, and some people think it is necessary to deal with their linguistic empiricism in order to keep up-to-date. There may even be some use in this procedure. Much to R.M. Hare's distaste, one could compare his *blik* with dogmatism's positing of a first principle. Similarly with Wisdom. But of course they did not mean it this way. They are all empiricists. Therefore, note the therefore, it is not really necessary to keep up-to-date. These men have added nothing essentially new to the older empiricism. Ramsey's models are as good as Hare's blik, even better. A dogmatist can agree with many of his sentences, though with few of his paragraphs, and with none of his chapters. All of

---

* *God and Other Minds,* pp. 167ff. Compare also, Everett W. Hall, "Metaphysics," in *Living Schools of Philosophy,* Dagobert D. Runes, ed., pp. 128ff., especially pp. 141-145.

these linguistic philosophers talk nonsense, but it seems to me that Ramsey's nonsense is the most intricate. Keith E. Yandell phrases it nicely: "If Ramsey's model is superior to Hume's or Descartes', he must prove it. In the absence of argument, the best he can claim is that he has insight where Hume was blind and Descartes misled."*

There must be first principles. A system cannot start unless it starts. The start is first. Therefore no one, since all must start somewhere, can consistently refuse permission to the dogmatist to start where he chooses.

Yet there is great opposition to this when it is a Christian dogmatist that claims the privilege. A typical example occurs in a widely used textbook. "The appeal to authority invests some sources with infallibility and finality and invokes some external force to give sanction to their decisions. . . . [T]he method of authority has been used to root out, as heretical or disloyal, divergent opinions."† When one remembers that certain institutions of higher learning used Hegelianism in the recent past to deny professorial standing to empiricists, and that other universities in the United States refused to employ any philosopher who was not a positivist, and that today there is strong objection to accepting a conservative Christian, sometimes even as a student, it will be recognized that Cohen and Nagel's rejection of authority is a propaganda device and not a valid argument. Nor do they themselves escape authority. No one can. The authority is their first principle, or it is they themselves. Everyone except the skeptic is an authoritarian. Even the least knowledge depends on a first principle.

---

* *Basic Issues in the Philosophy of Religion* (Allyn and Bacon, 1971), pp. 30-31.

† Cohen and Nagel, *An Introduction to Logic and Scientific Method* (New York: Harcourt, Brace and Co., 1934), p. 194.

Realism

There is a second similarity between rationalism and dogmatism. Anselm's ontological argument involved the principle that the mind is not limited to having a representation or image of God. A previous chapter pointed out that the common objection to the argument was the impossibility of passing from an image to a reality. But rationalism and dogmatism are forms of realism. Their epistemology is not representational.

Every thinker must decide for himself whether the X that is immediately in the mind is the real object or a representation of it. These who base knowledge on sensation have only two alternatives. They may, like Aristotle, assert that a sensory image is the result of and represents an external object. But in this case, as previously shown, there is no way to check the representation. Not only is it impossible to know whether or not the image is a faithful image; it is empirically impossible to know whether it represents anything at all. The second alternative is to deny the external object. Then we have images or sensations that represent nothing. They and they alone are the objects of knowledge. But in this case *you* cannot have *my* image any more than you can have my headache. No two of us can ever have the same thought because every thought is a purely personal experience. This makes communication impossible.

What is worse (or is it better?) there is no one to communicate with. Not only is it impossible to know another's thought, it is impossible to know that there is another. Each of us, or rather I alone know only my ideas, and what I call you is only one of my headaches. In technical language, empiricism results in solipsism. Even worse, it results in a solipsistic individual who can never know what he thought yesterday. There may have been images or sensations yesterday, but I can know only what is present to my mind. The past is unknowable. A present sensation and a past sensation are two different psychological events separated by a length of time. Not only are they different: I cannot show that they are even similar. Comparison requires the things compared both to be present. Thus the impossibility of knowing what is not present precludes all knowledge of the past. I cannot think the same object twice.

This second alternative may possibly be called realism in that the real, rather than some imitation or substitute for the real, is present to the mind; but it is a futile and useless realism. In fact a solipsistic individual, confined to the present, ignorant not only of yesterday's sensations but also of yesterday's self, hardly meets the requirements for being human.

Dogmatism is otherwise. It is neither representational nor non-representational nominalism. Nominalism is an impossible view anyway. In assuming that individual sense objects are the only realities, it not only founders on the skeptical implications of empiricism, it would in consistency require every noun to be a proper noun or name. We could call Timothy-Ticklepitchers by name, but we could not subsume him under the genus cat. Such a prohibition of universal concepts discourages conversation. Furthermore, when William of Occam and other medieval philosophers invented, or resurrected if you wish, nominalism, they naively supposed that sensory individuals could be identified. This cannot be done. Is a small stone on a mountainside the real individual, or is the mountain, or is it the mountain range? Those who take a firm stand on the stone run the risk of falling off when it crumbles into pebbles and then into atoms and then into protons or what not. Individuals are nowhere to be found.*

Thought and therefore intelligent conversation require something other than nominalistic proper nouns. This was the supreme triumph of Plato over the Pre-socratics. To be sure,

---

* Compare the *Festschrift, The Philosophy of Gordon H. Clark*, pp. 30ff.

Christian dogmatism does not accept the unaltered World of Platonic Ideas. The Philonic interpretation is better. Still better is the replacement of Ideas (minus predicates) by propositions or truths. But in any case nominalism is to be rejected.

Christian dogmatism therefore must be realistic. The real object of knowledge is itself present to the mind. One need not (one cannot) pass from an image to the truth. One knows the truth itself. The real object is not momentary. It is not something that cannot return. Sensations exist only once. When my headache no longer aches and when I no longer see blue or taste sweet, the aches and the sweet simply do not exist. As individual events they are over and done for. An individual sensation never occurs again. But a truth is not a sensation. It returns and I can think it again many times. Not only so, but you can have it too. Though I have it, though it is present to my mind, though it exists there, it is not so mine that you cannot have it too, at the same time. Your ache and mine can never be the same ache. Your truth and mine are identical.

These objects of knowledge are not trivialities such as blues and sweets. They are truths or propositions. An example, one of these realities, a constituent of the noumenal world, is the proposition that God justifies sinners on the basis of Christ's imputed righteousness. This is not only a thought to which I may return time and time again. It is also a thought you and I can have simultaneously. Thus communication as well as memory is possible.

There are of course other thoughts, objects, or realities. Every Biblical proposition is one. These never change nor go out of existence, for they are constituents of God's mind. Knowing them we know God. To know God, we do not pass from an unreal concept abstracted from sensory experience to a different reality. We know God directly, for in him we live and move and have our being.

Alternative Principles

All of this, naturally, depends on the acceptance of Biblical revelation. The secularists will have none of it. How can you prove, they ask, that the Bible is a divine revelation? Well, of course, a dogmatist does not try to prove it. The question ignores the preceding argument concerning skepticism, first principles, and suicide. There is, however, another question that secularists can ask and do. It is not an impertinent question. It raises an important issue the answer to which helps to clarify the dogmatic position. The question is: Granted that one must choose a first indemonstrable principle, how does one decide between two incompatible principles? Frederick Ferré saw the point. He wrote (*op. cit.*, p. 24), "Fortunately, however, we are not obliged to accept every position that is logically irrefutable. . . . The infinite class of gratuitous, irrefutable, but logically possible beliefs is also mutually inconsistent. Since what is not open to refutation may still be open to rejection, what shall we reply to the theological veto?" Ferré's answer is not very good, but the question is proper. The religious form of this philosophical question, the form that occurs in many a volume on religious types, the question hardly anyone fails to ask, is, Since several religions and several documents claim to be divinely revealed, how does one choose the Bible rather than the Koran?

This question properly understood and seriously put is not impertinent, as the first one was. Sometimes the difference is not understood, in which case it is taken as an objection to dogmatism. But it is not an objection. Nor should it be directed against dogmatism alone. Every non-skeptical position, as was made clear earlier, must have a first principle. Rationalists are well aware of this; empiricists usually ignore or deny it and claim presuppositionless objectivity. But it applies to them with equal force. They too must answer why they assign so basic a position to sensation. Hence there is a perfectly legitimate question, applicable to all types of philosophy, concerning the choice of a first principle.

Dogmatic Christianity has its answer, a clear-cut answer, to this impressive question. But to put it in perspective, one should briefly review some other answers.

The first of these answers, and one that at first seems to make a Christian claim, is Pascal's wager. It was described at the end of the preceding chapter. William James, neither a Christian nor a theist, paid it his sincere respects.

Pascal, of course, was a devout Christian; but his wager, although it escapes the accusation of irrationalism, is not the Christian answer to the problem. It is no answer at all to the problem, for it fails to explain a choice of the Bible rather than the Koran. A Moslem or presumably an exponent of any religion can equally well use Pascal's argument. But if a Moslem uses it, and says, Believe in Allah and the Koran, a Christian is likely to reply: Your risk is not zero by any means; if you win, you win nothing, for Allah is not God, and if you lose, you lose eternal life and suffer the just rewards of your sins. Therefore the basic question ought to have a better answer than Pascal's wager.

The problem also arises in science as well as religion. How does a scientist choose his first principle? Note well that he chooses or constructs it; he does not discover it.* Actually choice and construction occur in every minor law of physics, though some scientists still fail to recognize the fact. But in the supreme law or laws, the necessity of choice is more clearly seen. Even Cohen and Nagel *(op. cit.,* p. 215) base the most general laws of physics on "an incalculable esthetic element in the choice between rival theories." But if aesthetics is satisfactory for science, Christian dogmatism does not regard it as satisfactory for theology.

---

* Clark, *The Philosophy of Science and Belief in God.*

Before leaving the scientific situation completely behind, one must notice a most interesting and instructive admission by Herbert Feigl, prince of positivism. His *Logical Empiricism** begins:

> Probably the most decisive division among philosophical attitudes is the one between the worldly and the other-worldly types of thought. Profound differences in personality and temperament express themselves in the ever changing forms these two kinds of outlook assume. Very likely there is here an irreconcilable divergence. It goes deeper than disagreement in doctrine; at the bottom it is a difference in basic aim and interest. Countless frustrated discussions and controversies since antiquity testify that logical argument and empirical evidence are unable to resolve the conflict. In the last analysis this is so because the very issue of the jurisdictive power of the appeal to logic and experience (and with it the question of just what empirical evidence can establish) is at stake.
>
> It seems likely that this situation in philosophy will continue as long as human nature in its relations to its cultural environment remains what it has been for the last three or four thousand years. The tough-minded and the tender-minded, as William James described them so brilliantly, are perennial types, perennially antagonistic. There will always be those who find this world of ours, as cruel and deplorable as it may be in some respects, an exciting, fascinating place to live in, to explore, to adjust to, and to improve. And there will always be those who look upon the universe of experience and nature as an unimportant or secondary thing in comparison with something more fundamental and more significant. This tendency of thought may express itself theologically or metaphysically. It may lead to a faith in extra-mundane existence, or it may in various attentuated fashions assert merely the supremacy of some rational or intuitive principles.

---

* *Living Schools of Philosophy,* ed. Dagobert D. Runes, p. 325.

K.E. Yandell

Science is apt to avoid the problem of first principles. Discussions on religion cannot. Unfriendly critics press hard on it. More friendly volumes on the philosophy of religion frequently acknowledge it, but infrequently propose any definite solution. Usually it is left suspended in space. A fair and typical example, one even somewhat above the average, is that of Yandell's previously cited book, *Basic Issues in the Philosophy of Religion.*

The main part of Yandell's book, up to the last few pages, gives a penetrating analysis of many contemporary and some more ancient views. He pretty well explodes all the arguments against theism, and pretty well explodes all the arguments for theism. This is so well done that he should have expressed the skepticism of his conclusion more forcibly. At this point he might have tried to propose a first principle. He only raises the question as to how to choose one. These are his words (p. 226):

Conclusion. Although each of its chapters is hopefully sufficient unto itself, the present volume does present a sustained view of the philosophy of religion. This can be seen by summarizing its contentions. The fashionable contemporary claim that religious language is meaningless is supported by arguments quite insufficient to sustain their ambitious conclusion. Attempts to analyze religious discourse so that it involves no ontological claim, presupposes no description regarded as true of the Deity, turn out to be quite inadequate. The problem of evil, in its various formulations, does not refute traditional theism. Nor does the argument from contingency unambiguously support theism; similar comments apply to the teleological argument. Even less does the ontological argument prove its point. Religious experience provides no unequivocal evidence for religious claims. The moral argument is an articulation of morality within an already assumed theistic framework. Religious faith is an exhaustive interpretation of men and things in which they are regarded as created and providentially sustained by a Being worthy of complete devotion and obedience; this, at least, is the faith of traditional theism. Neither deductive proof from premises which are self-evident or empirically well supported, nor support via probability arguments, can vindicate this or any other interpretation. There are general characteristics in virtue of which exhaustive interpretations (in an older jargon, "world views") can be compared, and criteria by which they can be appraised. The task of appraisal is detailed, arduous, and unlikely to yield results agreed upon by all men of reason. Nonetheless, it is worth the effort. Making it is an effort in apologetics (positive or negative), a task neither necessarily biased nor intellectually despicable. The present work can be viewed, if one wishes, as a prolegomena to polemics. Its purpose has been to clarify the issues and resolve some of the preliminary problems. Its thesis, in part, is that the propositions at issue cannot properly be viewed in splendid isolation. Neither proof nor disproof is nearly so straightforward a process as is often supposed, and the battlelines on religious topics have often been drawn in the wrong places. The present effort, in part, is an attempt to redraw them.

Since the issues are important, our thought about them should be as clear as possible. Hopefully, the preceding will be of some help to that end. Even that is, of course, somewhat optimistic.

While the clarification of issues and the analysis of historic arguments are indispensable, they are disappointing without some constructive conclusion. The conclusion here to be proposed is very simple in itself. It provokes distaste because the opponents are still troubled by objections and because the progress of the argument and therefore the precise status of the solution is misunderstood.

Another Example

Within the ranks of evangelical Christianity in America this problem was interestingly exemplified, and there seems to be no good reason for a book on Dogmatism to avoid reference to the less scholarly travels of students and the more popular discussions in periodicals. Certain students from Westminster Seminary formed a sort of deputation team that visited (among other seminaries) Trinity Evangelical Divinity School. They presented a point of view that is at least somewhat similar to dogmatism as here defined. One of Trinity's brilliant and witty professors, John Warwick Montgomery, published an article in *Christianity Today* (March 31, 1972) entitled, "Having a Fuddled Easter?" It was a condemnation of the position in question.

Calling it "Fuddlement No. 3" and describing it as the thesis "Jesus rose in history, but you can't prove it," Dr. Montgomery wrote, "One might suppose that the documentary passage just cited [II Peter 1:16] would constitute, at least hypothetically, the kind of 'proof' that is marshalled for any historical event. 'No matter,' the orthodox presuppositionalists and pietists* inform us. 'You can't *prove* the resurrection. It's a matter of proper starting point and faith.' "

Rejecting this as "fuddled reasoning," Professor Montgomery, among other things, asks, "How would the presuppositionalist distinguish the Bible he claims to start with *apriori* from *Playboy* magazine?"

Three of the students who had visited Dr. Montgomery's seminary wrote letters in reply and *Christianity Today* published them (May 12, 1972). These three replies are quite good, although the first and third fail to state the crushing and basic consideration. The first letter, by Vern S. Poythress, states,

---

* A strange combination, since these two are so much at odds with each other.

> Historical judgments ought not to "lord it over the Gospel":
> the unbeliever may never be given the right to bring the Word of
> God into subjection to *his own* corrupt standards of truth. . . .
> There is nothing more sure than the Word of God, from which
> that Word now needs to be "proved" reliable. Christ the Son of
> the living God is more sure than any sense data or (secular)
> historical documents that we use scientifically.

Dogmatism applauds Mr. Poythress's assertion that there
is nothing more certain than the Word of God from which that
Word now needs to be proved. His repudiation of sense data is
quite in line with the preceding arguments in the preceding
sections of the present volume. These ideas are essential.
Nevertheless he compromises or weakens his position by
making or seeming to make the arguments against empiricism
depend on the corrupt mind of sinful man.

This flaw is even more clearly exemplified in the third
letter, by David W. King. He wrote,

> Unbelief . . . is not a problem of inadequate evidence or
> poorly argued logic; it is a matter of willful rebellion against the
> God of the facts. . . . The evidence abounds, from stars in
> heaven to the five hundred witnesses of I Corinthians 15:6—but
> men are not disposed to admit the evidence or able to weigh it
> until the Spirit unshackles the bonds of sin.

Once again this locates the difficulty in the sinful rebellion of
man against God. But this misses the main point.

The second letter, by Paul S. Andrews, is more perceptive.
It reads,

> The issue is not historicity or possibility of proof, as
> Montgomery claims; rather it is the question of the propriety of
> basing one's apologetics on these foundations without taking
> into account the presuppositions of the natural man. . . .
> [Presuppositionalists] challenge the idea of a neutral reasoning

and show clearly the Christian confidence in the law of non-contradiction as over against the non-believer's concept of the same.

The wording here seems to indicate that Mr. Andrews denies that there is any such thing as neutral reasoning, and he emphasizes foundations, presuppositions, or starting points. All this is excellent.

Nevertheless, contrary to what Mr. Andrews says, the issue is indeed the possibility of proof. In this particular the letter has misunderstood Dr. Montgomery. The fact of sin is really irrelevant. Those who stress human depravity in this argument give the impression that Adam before the fall was, and the elect in heaven will be, able to construct valid arguments, based on sensations, to prove the veracity of God. But the crushing and basic reply to the Montgomery position is that all inductive arguments are formal fallacies. Historical arguments to prove the resurrection and all sensory arguments to prove its significance are as bad as and indeed worse than trying to prove that a triangle contains two right angles by measuring a half a dozen drawn triangles with a protractor. The method is impossible, and it is as impossible for an innocent Adam as for guilty Barabbas. Sin cannot make a valid argument fallacious, nor can perfect righteousness make a fallacy valid.

In addition to this basic material touched upon in these letters one may note also that Dr. Montgomery seems to have been a little unfortunate in wording some of his objections. He asserted that if a theologian assents to an apriori first principle, he cannot then "distinguish the Bible he claims to start with *apriori* from *Playboy* magazine."

Since it is easier to distinguish the difference between Christianity and *Playboy's* obscenities than it is to distinguish Riemannian from Euclidean geometry, wisdom counsels us to rephrase the objection, to state what Dr. Montgomery intended to state, and then to answer what he meant but did not say. What he obviously meant was that apriori principles, since they are not based on evidence, are arbitrary; and if arbitrary, the apriori of *Playboy* is just as legitimate as the fundamental principles of Christianity. Now, there is a certain sense in which this is true enough. If neither set of principles can be based on evidence, and if both sets are regarded by their advocates as the starting point for all demonstration and argument, then obviously no one can support either set on anything more fundamental. This is simply to say that every system of thought must start somewhere.

Where then does Dr. Montgomery start? So far as I can understand him, he professes to base the truth of the Bible on archaeological and historical evidence. This evidence in turn is based on sensation or perception. Or, more philosophically, one may classify Dr. Montgomery as an empiricist. As such he must hold that sensory experience is more reliable than a divinely given revelation. He must hold that sensation is self-authenticating and that the Bible cannot be self-authenticating.

No doubt somewhere in the argument he will ask, How can you convince an unbeliever if you start with the Bible? It is the truth of the Bible of which you wish to convince the unbeliever. Therefore you cannot start with what you wish to prove. Furthermore, Dr. Montgomery will continue, in order to convince someone of something, is it not necessary to start with something he already admits? Since he does not admit the truth of the Bible, obviously an evangelist must start with something else.

The dogmatist, on the other hand, can as easily ask, How can Dr. Montgomery convince a dogmatist of archaeology if he does not accept the first principle of empiricism? With all the difficulties attaching to sensation that this volume has already detailed, it is hard to maintain that sensation is self-authenticating and the Bible is not. Since the empiricist is as much a "dogmatist" on sensation as the consistent Christian is on revelation, Dr. Montgomery is equally unable to provide any evidence for his own first principle. He failed to convince the three Westminster students. The reason he failed is that what he calls evidence is evidence only on his presuppositions as to what the nature of evidence is. Therefore the objections he levels against presuppositionalism apply to himself with equal force.

Before the explanation is given on how the dogmatist may convince an unbeliever of the truth of Christianity without using sensory evidence, it is interesting to note that Dr. Montgomery's actual procedure is (dogmatically) better than his empirical theory. A page or two ago the reader noted that Dr. Montgomery said, "One might suppose that the documentary passage just cited [II Peter 1:16] would constitute, at least hypothetically, the kind of proof that is marshalled for any historical event." In this Dr. Montgomery appeals to the veracity of Peter. At least the present writer hopes he (inconsistently) makes this appeal, for this would seem to be the correct Christian procedure. It is an appeal to divine revelation. True enough, the sentence quoted can mean something else more in accord with Dr. M's theory. The sentence says that the verse in II Peter is "the kind of proof that is marshalled for any historical event" by any secular historian. The present writer, however, does not believe that an appeal to this verse is the kind of proof the secular historians use. But if it be so taken, then one must search for a mass of evidences, archaeological evidences, second century evidences, any extra-biblical evidences to prove that it was Peter who spoke and that he spoke the truth. Note well that the evidence would have to establish a first century date and an apostolic author, but also it would have to establish that the apostle spoke the truth. Secular assumptions forbid us to take the veracity of apostles on faith. It must be proved independently for every verse. This secular process never arrives validly at the veracity of Peter: In fact it never arrives validly at anything. Therefore a dogmatist must hope that his respected friend became inconsistent at the crucial point by appealing to revelation.

The End of Investigation

Somewhere in the voluminous first *Critque* Kant complains, and the complaint has been echoed many times since, that theism puts an end to further investigation: If a phenomenon is referred directly to the will of God, no room is left to examine its antecedents and concomitants. Though this objection impresses some people, it has little logical force because the acceptance of a law of physics, just as much as the acceptance of divine providence, puts an end to further investigation. When the seventeenth-century physicists investigated the phenomena of the pendulum, they stopped when they formulated the law. In this respect belief in a law of physics and belief in God are on a par. Kant may claim that he can still check his old experiments, can even formulate another law, or certainly go on to other problems connected somehow with the pendulum. But all this implies that he has not definitely accepted the law. A religionist too can reexamine his belief in God, perhaps formulate a humanistic theory to take its place, and can surely at least consider other instances of providence. But so long as belief is confidently held, one does not continue to re-solve the solution. When one believes that he has solved a problem, further investigation of that point is at an end. The objection is poor therefore because it applies to theology no more than to physics.

On a more popular level, a level not quite so basic, Kant's criticism of theology seems to cover two situations, in one of which the complaint is true, while in the other it is false. The latter is exemplified in the escape of the Israelites from their slavery in Egypt. When God sent a strong east wind to blow back the waters of the Red Sea, it remained possible to investigate the force of winds on waters. Here belief in God does not put an end to investigation. However, the type of case to which the complaint does not apply seems to merge gradually into a situation where it holds. To return to the example, though it is possible to continue to investigate the force of wind on water, yet if God sent the wind, is there room to investigate the cause of winds? If God produced the winds by moving hot desert air, can the motion of the air be further explained? Somewhere in this regressive series God acts directly and immediately, and there the regress ends. Investigation may continue a long way back, but certainly it must end at creation. If God created the universe, if therefore the world has a temporal beginning, if no state of the world preceded, obviously investigation must stop. But, so the argument claims, regress must never be permitted to end. Never. One is not even allowed the judicious amendment by the Captain of the Pinafore. For this would be tantamount to admitting the existence of God.

This objection does not apply only to theism. Any system ends its regress in its first principle. This may not be a temporal end to regress, but it certainly puts an end to further explanation. Chemical change can be explained on the atomic theory, then atoms are explained by protons, and finally all is reduced to mystic Energy. Here explanation ends. Of course a different system may someday be proposed, but it too will have an end. An explanation of a subsidiary phenomenon depends on a more general principle, until Kant's own investigation ends in the categories. These are final. Are there no final answers? Must explanatory regress never end? Then we again have the skepticism that prevents us from even recognizing wind and water in the first place. Thus if there is a final answer or a first principle, investigation must stop somewhere; but if there is no final answer, there is no knowledge out of which to construct the objection.

This is why Lessing's famous remark is so silly. He said that if God offered him either the truth or the activity of searching for truth and never finding it, he would choose the latter. Now if life is a mere game, there is a superficial plausibility that playing is more fun than winning. Athletes, however, prefer to win. And it seems silly to seek earnestly, and with some trouble, an object you know cannot be found. Yet there are university professors today who are so enamored of academic freedom and so devoted to an endless search for truth that they are antagonistic to those who say they have found some. Possessing truth, in their view, is a violation of academic freedom.

But there is a more compelling refutation of Lessing. He prefers endless search over successful discovery—why? No doubt because it is more fun. And a life of fun, or some more professorial term, is the highest good. Lessing therefore prefers endless, unsuccessful search because he has already terminated his search for the highest good. He has found the final and absolute truth that search is more fun than finding. Dogmatism is at least more honest in stating unambiguously that its search has ended.

The End of Communication

There is another and final objection to dogmatism. This type of philosophy, so its critics claim, is to be rejected because it puts an end to communication and eliminates all possibility of convincing an opponent. Anselm adopted his form of rationalism because he thought it enabled him to meet Jews and Moslems on the common ground of "reason." Recall the quotation in the *Introduction* of the present work. Part of it was, "Leaving Christ out of view, as if nothing had ever been known of him, it *[Cur Deus Homo]* proves by absolute reasons the impossibility that any man should be saved without him." The death of the God-Man must be proved "reasonable and necessary," so as to convince one "unwilling to believe anything not previously proved by reason." Similarly in the *Monologium* he says, "In order that nothing in Scripture should be urged on the authority of Scripture itself, but that whatever the conclusion of independent investigation should declare to be true, should, in an unadorned style, with common proofs and with a simple argument, be briefly enforced by the cogency of reason and plainly expounded in the light of truth." As Anselm wanted to convert the Moslems, so today evangelical empiricists want to convert humanists by arguments based on some common principles, such as the trustworthiness of sensation.

Because dogmatism is an all inclusive system and has no propositions in common with any other system, its Christian opponents throw up their hands in despair and whimper, How then can we recommend the doctrines of Christ to anyone? Agreement at some point must, they say, indeed *must* be found, if one person is to convince another. Is this not the way ordinary conversation is carried on? When I want to persuade you to have lunch with me, I appeal to premises on which we agree: that lunch is good, that our conversation will be profitable or enjoyable, that we have to eat now anyway, etc., etc. Or, more academically, I convince you that the square of the hypotenuse equals the other two on the basis of axioms we both accept. If you did not agree with my axioms, I could not convince you. Now, in dogmatism, a Christian cannot convince a Moslem because there is no agreement. The one accepts the Bible, the other the Koran. Since both are dogmatists, neither can appeal to higher common principles.

All this sounds very plausible, and the reference to the Moslems and the Koran is very true. Nevertheless, logically, it is a poor objection to dogmatism because it applies with equal force against, not only Anselm, but even the contemporary evangelical empiricists who use it with such an air of finality. Let us ask, in all seriousness, How can a Logical Positivist convince me, Christian Dogmatist that I am, that sensory experience is the sole test both of truth and meaning? Can a Christian empiricist, who presumably rejects the second part of the positivists' thesis but retains the first, appeal to the Bible to convince me that only in sensation is the basis of truth to be found? He certainly cannot appeal to sensation to prove the truth of sensation when the truth of sensation is the very point at issue. Two persons who agree on their axioms can in this way solve subsidiary problems. But the status of the argument now confronts us with the selection of axioms or choice of first principles. This difficulty is found in every system, and the empiricist does not compliment his intelligence by raising it as an objection against dogmatism. Let us without reluctance acknowledge that Feigl at this point understood more clearly than most of his fellow empiricists.

If now one appreciates the present status of the argument, the dogmatic answer to the question can easily be given. The present status of the argument is the choice between dogmatism and nihilism. Empiricism has been demolished. Unless therefore one chooses a dogmatic first principle, one must choose skepticism and irrationality. Neither of these has anything to oppose to dogmatism. Sanity therefore must be dogmatic. So much then for the status of the argument.

What now is the question to be answered? It is not, Shall we choose? Or, is it permissible to choose? We must choose; since we are alive we have chosen—either a dogmatic principle or empirical insanity. The question therefore, urged by atheist, evangelical Christian, and evangelistic Moslem, is, Why does anyone choose the Bible rather than the Koran? The answer to this question will also explain how a Christian can present the Gospel to a non-Christian without depending on any logically common proposition in their two systems.

Since all possible knowledge must be contained within the system and deduced from its principles, the dogmatic answer must be found in the Bible itself. The answer is that faith is the gift of God. As Psalm 65:4 says, God chooses a man and causes him to accept Christian dogmatism. Conversely, the Apostle John informs us that the Pharisees could not believe because God had blinded their eyes and hardened their hearts.

The initiation of spiritual life, called regeneration, is the immediate work of the Holy Spirit. It is not produced by

Abrahamic blood, nor by natural desire, nor by any act of human will. In particular, it is not produced by arguments based on secular and empirical presuppositions. Even if there were a common truth in secularism and Christianity, arguments based on it would not produce faith. What empirical evangelicals think is most necessary, is most useless.

Even the preaching of the Gospel does not produce faith. However, the preaching of the Gospel does one thing that a fallacious argument from a non-existent common ground cannot do: It provides the propositions that must be believed. But the belief comes from God, God causes a man to believe; faith is a divine gift. In evangelistic work there can be no appeal to secular, non-Christian material. There is an appeal—it is the appeal of prayer to the Holy Spirit to cause the sinner to accept the truths of the Gospel. Any other appeal is useless.

If now a person wants the basic answer to the question, Why does one man have faith and another not, or, Why does one man accept the Koran and another the Bible, this is it. God causes the one to believe. But if a person asks some other question or raises an objection, he will have to read the argument over again.

Note on *Ad Hominem* Tactics

Empirical evangelicals sometimes, usually, logically without exception, regard dogmatism as condemning the Christian apologist to archaeological silence. If historical investigation at best could corroborate the truth of only this or that Biblical passage and not the inspiration and truth of all Scripture, and if at worst, *i.e.* technically and accurately, empiricism cannot guarantee the reliability of perception, leaving in doubt the description of an artifact and even its natural status, does not the dogmatic Christian deprive himself of the tremendous advangage of using these startling discoveries in his evangelistic endeavors? This question, with its presupposed, unargued, affirmative answer is thought to cover the dogmatist with inescapable ridicule.

The dogmatist, however, can make two replies. One is basic and in a way repeats the argument already given in the body of this book, merely applying it to this particular case. The second is more tactical to suit less philosophical tastes.

Briefly the first reply seizes upon the rhetorical nature of the question. The form of the question presupposes an affirmative answer. It tacitly excludes a negative answer. It is at the same time a disguised double question (like, Have you stopped beating your wife yet?), and as such hides a dogmatic assertion that empiricists on their theory ought to eschew. Or, to put it another way, it assumes without reasons that perception can indeed accurately describe artifacts and that a thinker can validly draw from them the conclusion that Christianity is true. If it were a fact that perception is accurate, the question would be legitimate. If the reverse is the case, there are no materials with which to frame the question. That is to say, the question itself assumes the points at issue and is thus merely an illogical device to avoid facing the argument.

The nonphilosophical public, however, is unquestioningly sure that silence on archaeology is ridiculous. Arguments or no arguments, reasons or no reasons, philosophy or no philosophy, archaeology can be spoken about. This is more certain than the academic pretension that sensation might be mistaken. Why pay attention to addled egg-heads?

Now, it may come as a surprise to some empiricists that nothing in this book precludes talking about archaeology. Further, the method of talking about archaeology will be satisfactory to the non-philosophical public, even though dogmatic empiricists may sputter somewhat. But then they have no business concerning themselves with this second reply before they have escaped the stringencies of the first.

The second reply is that dogmatism allows a person to use *ad hominem* arguments for what they are worth. And they are worth the embarrassment they create for liberal theologians.

To illustrate: Two books before me assert that Moses could not have written the Pentateuch because no such claim is made on its pages. Some other books assert that seven-stemmed lamps were first invented during the late Persian period, and hence their mention in Exodus 37 shows that Exodus was written in post-exilic times.

Ordinarily an apologete would reply that Caesar's *Gallic War* contains no claim of Caesarian authorship and that in 1962 the archaeologists dug up a seven-stemmed lamp dating many centuries before the time of Moses.

Such a reply is what the non-academic Christian wants made. But the academic empiricist complains that on the dogmatist's theory the dogmatist has no right to make such a reply. And such surely seems to be the case at first glance.

The dogmatic solution of the paradox lies in the fact that his archaeological reply was directed to the liberal theologian in an ordinary conversation. If, however, there is an empiricist present who needs to be satisfied, the ordinary reply must be expanded by making explicit some of the unexpressed conditions. Accordingly the dogmatist would say: Sir, you accept (do you not?) the scientific norms of historiography as they are used by contemporary secular historians. The liberal nods his head. Then how is it, the dogmatist continues, you doubt or deny the Mosaic authorship of Exodus, but do not challenge Caesar's? How is it you apply a norm to Exodus and refrain from applying it to the *Gallic War?* Or, in the same way, the dogmatist would say: Sir, you agree (do you not?) that the method of dating by means of pottery is exceedingly accurate. Then how can you maintain that Moses could not have described seven-stemmed lamps when you admit they were in use in Abraham's times?

Now, perhaps, an actual discussion would be longer than the preceding paragraph, but the dogmatic mode of argument is clear. It consists of an *ad hominem* attempt to convict the liberal of contradicting himself. The dogmatist does not attempt to prove the reliability of pottery dating, nor the contemporary principles of historiography. He is not really interested in them. In fact, he has, to his own satisfaction at least, shown that they are indefensible and untenable. But none of this vitiates his attempt to convict the liberal of self-contradiction. And covered with contradiction, the liberal and the empiricist, not the dogmatist, have been reduced to silence. Once this is done, there remain no empirical objections against the truth of Scripture. The apologetic task is completed.

Index

Scripture Index

The Crisis of Our Time

Historians have christened the thirteenth century the Age of Faith and termed the eighteenth century the Age of Reason. The twentieth century has been called many things: the Atomic Age, the Age of Inflation, the Age of the Tyrant, the Age of Aquarius. But it deserves one name more than the others: the Age of Irrationalism. Contemporary secular intellectuals are anti-intellectual. Contemporary philosophers are anti-philosophy. Contemporary theologians are anti-theology.

In past centuries secular philosophers have generally believed that knowledge is possible to man. Consequently they expended a great deal of thought and effort trying to justify knowledge. In the twentieth century, however, the optimism of the secular philosophers has all but disappeared. They despair of knowledge.

Like their secular counterparts, the great theologians and doctors of the church taught that knowledge is possible to man. Yet the theologians of the twentieth century have repudiated that belief. They also despair of knowledge. This radical skepticism has filtered down from the philosophers and theologians and penetrated our entire culture, from television to music to literature. *The Christian in the twentieth century is confronted with an overwhelming cultural consensus—sometimes stated explicitly, but most often implicitly: Man does not and cannot know anything truly.*

What does this have to do with Christianity? Simply this: If man can know nothing truly, man can truly know nothing. We cannot know that the Bible is the Word of God, that Christ died for sin, or that Christ is alive today at the right hand of the Father. Unless knowledge is possible, Christianity is nonsensical, for it claims to be knowledge. What is at stake in the twentieth century is not simply a single doctrine, such as the Virgin Birth, or the existence of hell, as important as those doctrines may be, but the whole of Christianity itself. If knowledge is not possible to man, it is worse than silly to argue points of doctrine—it is insane.

The irrationalism of the present age is so thorough-going and pervasive that even the Remnant—the segment of the professing church that remains faithful—has accepted much of it, frequently without even being aware of what it was accepting. In some circles this irrationalism has become synonymous with piety and humility, and those who oppose it are denounced as rationalists—as though to be logical were a sin. Our contemporary anti-theologians make a contradiction and call it a Mystery. The faithful ask for truth and are given Paradox. If any balk at swallowing the absurdities of the anti-theologians, they are frequently marked as heretics or schismatics who seek to act independently of God.

There is no greater threat facing the true Church of Christ at this moment than the irrationalism that now controls our entire culture. Communism, guilty of tens of millions of murders, including those of millions of Christians, is to be feared, but not nearly so much as the idea that we do not and cannot know the truth. Hedonism, the popular philosophy of America, is not to be feared so much as the belief that logic —that "mere human logic," to use the religious irrationalists' own phrase—is futile. The attacks on truth, on revelation, on the intellect, and on logic are renewed daily. But note well: The misologists—the haters of logic—use logic to demonstrate the futility of using logic. The anti-intellectuals construct intricate intellectual arguments to prove the insufficiency of the intellect. The anti-theologians use the revealed Word of God to show that there can be no revealed Word of God—or that if there could, it would remain impenetrable darkness and Mystery to our finite minds.

Nonsense Has Come

Is it any wonder that the world is grasping at straws—the straws of experientialism, mysticism and drugs? After all, if people are told that the Bible contains insoluble mysteries, then is not a flight into mysticism to be expected? On what grounds can it be condemned? Certainly not on logical grounds or Biblical grounds, if logic is futile and the Bible unintelligible. Moreover, if it cannot be condemned on logical or Biblical grounds, it cannot be condemned at all. If people are going to have a religion of the mysterious, they will not adopt Christianity: They will have a genuine mystery religion. "Those who call for Nonsense," C.S. Lewis once wrote, "will find that it comes." And that is precisely what has happened. The popularity of Eastern mysticism, of drugs, and of religious experience is the logical consequence of the irrationalism of the twentieth century. There can and will be no Christian revival—and no reconstruction of society—unless and until the irrationalism of the age is totally repudiated by Christians.

The Church Defenseless

Yet how shall they do it? The spokesmen for Christianity have been fatally infected with irrationalism. The seminaries, which annually train thousands of men to teach millions of Christians, are the finishing schools of irrationalism, completing the job begun by the government schools and colleges. Some of the pulpits of the most conservative churches (we are not speaking of the apostate churches) are occupied by graduates of the anti-theological schools. These products of modern anti-theological education, when asked to give a reason for the hope that is in them, can generally respond with only the intellectual analogue of a shrug—a mumble about Mystery. They have not grasped—and therefore cannot teach those for whom they are responsible—the first truth: "And ye shall know the truth." Many, in fact, explicitly deny it, saying that, at best, we possess only "pointers" to the truth, or something "similar" to the truth, a mere analogy. Is the impotence of the Christian Church a puzzle? Is the fascination with pentecostalism and faith healing among members of conservative churches an enigma? Not when one understands the sort of studied nonsense that is purveyed in the name of God in the seminaries.

The Trinity Foundation

The creators of The Trinity Foundation firmly believe that theology is too important to be left to the licensed theologians —the graduates of the schools of theology. They have created The Trinity Foundation for the express purpose of teaching the faithful all that the Scriptures contain—not warmed over, baptized, secular philosophies. Each member of the board of directors of The Trinity Foundation has signed this oath: "I believe that the Bible alone and the Bible in its entirety is the Word of God and, therefore, inerrant in the autographs. I believe that the system of truth presented in the Bible is best summarized in the Westminster Confession of Faith. So help me God."

The ministry of The Trinity Foundation is the presentation of the system of truth taught in Scripture as clearly and as completely as possible. We do not regard obscurity as a virtue, nor confusion as a sign of spirituality. Confusion, like all error, is sin, and teaching that confusion is all that Christians can hope for is doubly sin.

The presentation of the truth of Scripture necessarily involves the rejection of error. The Foundation has exposed and will continue to expose the irrationalism of the twentieth century, whether its current spokesman be an existentialist philosopher or a professed Reformed theologian. We oppose anti-intellectualism, whether it be espoused by a neo-orthodox theologian or a fundamentalist evangelist. We reject misology, whether it be on the lips of a neo-evangelical or those of a Roman Catholic charismatic. To each error we bring the brilliant light of Scripture, proving all things, and holding fast to that which is true.

The Primacy of Theory

The ministry of The Trinity Foundation is not a "practical" ministry. If you are a pastor, we will not enlighten you on how to organize an ecumenical prayer meeting in your community or how to double church attendance in a year. If you are a homemaker, you will have to read elsewhere to find out how to become a total woman. If you are a businessman, we will not tell you how to develop a social conscience. The professing church is drowning in such "practical" advice.

The Trinity Foundation is unapologetically theoretical in its outlook, believing that theory without practice is dead, and that practice without theory is blind. The trouble with the professing church is not primarily in its practice, but in its theory. Christians do not know, and many do not even care to know, the doctrines of Scripture. Doctrine is intellectual, and Christians are generally anti-intellectual. Doctrine is ivory tower philosophy, and they scorn ivory towers. The ivory tower, however, is the control tower of a civilization. It is a fundamental, theoretical mistake of the practical men to think that they can be merely practical, for practice is always the practice of some theory. The relationship between theory and practice is the relationship between cause and effect. If a person believes correct theory, his practice will tend to be correct. The practice of contemporary Christians is immoral because it is the practice of false theories. It is a major theoretical mistake of the practical men to think that they can ignore the ivory towers of the philosophers and theologians as irrelevant to their lives. Every action that the "practical" men take is governed by the thinking that has occurred in some ivory tower—whether that tower be the British Museum, the Academy, a home in Basel, Switzerland, or a tent in Israel.

In Understanding Be Men

It is the first duty of the Christian to understand correct theory—correct doctrine—and thereby implement correct practice. This order—first theory, then practice—is both logical and Biblical. It is, for example, exhibited in Paul's epistle to the Romans, in which he spends the first eleven chapters expounding theory and the last five discussing practice. The contemporary teachers of Christians have not only reversed the order, they have inverted the Pauline emphasis on theory and practice. The virtually complete failure of the teachers of the professing church to instruct the faithful in correct doctrine is the cause of the misconduct and cultural impotence of Christians. The Church's lack of power is the result of its lack of truth. The *Gospel* is the power of God, not religious experience or personal relationship. The Church has no power because it has abandoned the Gospel, the good news, for a religion of experientialism. Twentieth century American Christians are children carried about by every wind of doctrine, not knowing what they believe, or even if they believe anything for certain.

The chief purpose of The Trinity Foundation is to counteract the irrationalism of the age and to expose the errors of the teachers of the church. Our emphasis—on the Bible as the sole source of truth, on the primacy of the intellect, on the supreme importance of correct doctrine, and on the necessity for systematic and logical thinking—is almost unique in Christendom. To the extent that the church survives—and she will survive and flourish—it will be because of her increasing acceptance of these basic ideas and their logical implications.

We believe that the Trinity Foundation is filling a vacuum in Christendom. We are saying that Christianity is intellectually defensible—that, in fact, it is the only intellectually defensible system of thought. We are saying that God has made the wisdom of this world—whether that wisdom be called science, religion, philosophy, or common sense—foolishness. We are appealing to all Christians who have not conceded defeat in the intellectual battle with the world to join us in our efforts to raise a standard to which all men of sound mind can repair.

The love of truth, of God's Word, has all but disappeared in our time. We are committed to and pray for a great instauration. But though we may not see this reformation of Christendom in our lifetimes, we believe it is our duty to present the whole counsel of God because Christ has commanded it. The results of our teaching are in God's hands, not ours. Whatever those results, His Word is never taught in vain, but always accomplishes the result that He intended it to accomplish. Professor Gordon H. Clark has stated our view well:

There have been times in the history of God's people, for example, in the days of Jeremiah, when refreshing grace and widespread revival were not to be expected: the time was one of chastisement. If this twentieth century is of a similar nature, individual Christians here and there can find comfort and strength in a study of God's Word. But if God has decreed happier days for us and if we may expect a world-shaking and genuine spiritual awakening, then it is the author's belief that a zeal for souls, however necessary, is not the sufficient condition. Have there not been devout saints in every age, numerous enough to carry on a revival? Twelve such persons are plenty. What distinguishes the arid ages from the period of the Reformation, when nations were moved as they had not been since Paul preached in Ephesus, Corinth, and Rome, is the latter's fullness of knowledge of God's Word. To echo an early Reformation thought, when the ploughman and the garage attendant know the Bible as well as the theologian does, and know it better than some contemporary theologians, then the desired awakening shall have already occurred.

In addition to publishing books, of which *Three Types of Religious Philosophy* is the twenty-first, the Foundation publishes a bimonthly newsletter, *The Trinity Review.* Subscriptions to *The Review* are free; please write to the address below to become a subscriber. If you would like further information or would like to join us in our work, please let us know.

The Trinity Foundation is a non-profit foundation tax-exempt under section 501 (c)(3) of the Internal Revenue Code of 1954. You can help us disseminate the Word of God through your tax-deductible contributions to the Foundation.

And we know that the Son of God is come, and hath given us an understanding, that we may know him that is true, and we are in him that is true, in his Son Jesus Christ. This is the true God, and eternal life.

John W. Robbins
President

Intellectual Ammunition

The Trinity Foundation is committed to the reconstruction of philosophy and theology along Biblical lines. We regard God's command to bring all our thoughts into conformity with Christ very seriously, and the books listed below are designed to accomplish that goal. They are written with two subordinate purposes: (1) to demolish all secular claims to knowledge; and (2) to build a system of truth based upon the Bible alone.

Works of Philosophy

Answer to Ayn Rand, John W. Robbins $4.95
   The only analysis and criticism of the views of novelist-philosopher Ayn Rand from a consistently Christian perspective.

Behaviorism and Christianity, Gordon H. Clark $5.95
   Behaviorism *is a critique of both secular and religious behaviorists. It includes chapters on John Watson, Edgar S. Singer Jr., Gilbert Ryle, B.F. Skinner, and Donald MacKay. Clark's refutation of behaviorism and his argument for a Christian doctrine of man are unanswerable.*

A Christian Philosophy of Education, Gordon H. Clark $8.95
   The first edition of this book was published in 1946. It sparked the contemporary interest in Christian schools. Dr. Clark has thoroughly revised and updated it, and it is needed now more than ever. Its chapters include: The Need for a World-View, The Christian World-View, The Alternative to Christian Theism, Neutrality, Ethics, The Christian

Philosophy of Education, Academic Matters, Kindergarten to University. Three appendices are included as well: The Relationship of Public Education to Christianity, A Protestant World-View, and Art and the Gospel.

A Christian View of Men and Things, Gordon H. Clark $8.95
No other book achieves what A Christian View *does: the presentation of Christianity as it applies to history, politics, ethics, science, religion, and epistemology. Clark's command of both worldly philosophy and Scripture is evident on every page, and the result is a breathtaking and invigorating challenge to the wisdom of this world.*

Clark Speaks From The Grave, Gordon H. Clark $3.95
Dr. Clark chides some of his critics for their failure to defend Christianity competently. Clark Speaks *is a stimulating and illuminating discussion of the errors of contemporary apologists.*

Education, Christianity, and the State $7.95
J. Gresham Machen
Machen was one of the foremost educators, theologians, and defenders of Christianity in the twentieth century. The author of numerous scholarly books, Machen saw clearly that if Christianity is to survive and flourish, a system of Christian grade schools must be established. This collection of essays captures his thought on education over nearly three decades.

Logic, Gordon H. Clark $8.95
Written as a textbook for Christian schools, Logic *is another unique book from Clark's pen. His presentation of the laws of thought, which must be followed if Scripture is to be understood correctly, and which are found in Scripture itself, is both clear and thorough.* Logic *is an indispensable book for the thinking Christian.*

The Philosophy of Science and Belief in God $5.95
Gordon H. Clark
In opposing the contemporary idolatry of science, Clark analyzes three major aspects of science: the problem of motion, Newtonian science, and modern theories of physics. His conclusion is that science,

while it may be useful, is always false; and he demonstrates its falsity in numerous ways. Since science is always false, it can offer no objection to the Bible and Christianity.

Religion, Reason and Revelation, Gordon H. Clark $7.95
One of Clark's apologetical masterpieces, Religion, Reason and Revelation has been praised for the clarity of its thought and language. It includes chapters on Is Christianity a Religion? Faith and Reason, Inspiration and Language, Revelation and Morality, and God and Evil. It is must reading for all serious Christians.

Selections from Hellenistic Philosophy, Gordon H. Clark $10.95
This is one of Clark's early works in which he translates, edits, and comments upon works by the Epicureans, the Stoics, Plutarch, Philo Judaeus, Hermes Trismegistus, and Plotinus. First published in 1940, it has been a standard college text for more than four decades.

William James, Gordon H. Clark $2.00
America has not produced many philosophers, but William James has been extremely influential. Clark examines his philosophy of Pragmatism.

Works of Theology

The Atonement, Gordon H. Clark $8.95
This is a major addition to Clark's multi-volume systematic theology. In The Atonement, *Clark discusses the Covenants, the Virgin Birth and Incarnation, federal headship and representation, the relationship between God's sovereignty and justice, and much more. He analyzes traditional views of the Atonement and criticizes them in the light of Scripture alone.*

The Biblical Doctrine of Man, Gordon H. Clark $5.95
Is man soul and body or soul, spirit, and body? What is the image of God? Is Adam's sin imputed to his children? Is evolution true? Are men

totally depraved? What is the heart? These are some to the questions discussed and answered from Scripture in this book.

Cornelius Van Til: The Man and The Myth $2.45
John W. Robbins
The actual teachings of this eminent Philadelphia theologian have been obscured by the myths that surround him. This book penetrates those myths and criticizes Van Til's surprisingly unorthodox views of God and the Bible.

Faith and Saving Faith, Gordon H. Clark $5.95
The views of the Roman Catholic church, John Calvin, Thomas Manton, John Owen, Charles Hodge, and B.B. Warfield are discussed in this book. Is the object of faith a person or a proposition? Is faith more than belief? Is belief more than thinking with assent, as Augustine said? In a world chaotic with differing views of faith, Clark clearly explains the Biblical view of faith and saving faith.

God's Hammer: The Bible and Its Critics, Gordon H. Clark $6.95
The starting point of Christianity, the doctrine on which all other doctrines depend, is "The Bible alone is the Word of God written, and therefore inerrant in the autographs." Over the centuries the opponents of Christianity, with Satanic shrewdness, have concentrated their attacks on the truthfulness and completeness of the Bible. In the twentieth century the attack is not so much in the fields of history and archaeology as in philosophy. Clark's brilliant defense of the complete truthfulness of the Bible is captured in this collection of eleven major essays.

The Incarnation, Gordon H. Clark $8.95
Who was Christ? The attack on the Incarnation in the nineteenth and twentieth centuries has been vigorous, but the orthodox response has been lame. Clark reconstructs the doctrine of the Incarnation building upon and improving upon the Chalcedonian definition.

In Defense of Theology, Gordon H. Clark $12.95
There are four groups to whom Clark addresses this book: the average Christians who are uninterested in theology, the atheists and agnostics, the religious experientalists, and the serious Christians. The

vindication of the knowledge of God against the objections of three of these groups is the first step in theology.

Logical Criticisms of Textual Criticism, Gordon H. Clark $2.95
In this critique of the science of textual criticism, Dr. Clark exposes the fallacious argumentation of the modern textual critics and defends the view that the early Christians knew better than the modern critics which manuscripts of the New Testament were more accurate.

Pat Robertson: A Warning to America, John W. Robbins $6.95
The Protestant Reformation was based on the Biblical principle that the Bible is the only revelation from God, yet a growing political-religious movement, led by Pat Robertson, asserts that God speaks to them directly. This book addresses the serious issue of religious fanaticism in America by examining the theological and political views of Presidential candidate Pat Robertson.

Predestination, Gordon H. Clark $7.95
Clark thoroughly discusses one of the most controversial and pervasive doctrines of the Bible: that God is, quite literally, Almighty. Free will, the origin of evil, God's omniscience, creation, and the new birth are all presented within a Scriptural framework. The objections of those who do not believe in the Almighty God are considered and refuted. This edition also contains the text of the booklet, Predestination in the Old Testament.

Scripture Twisting in the Seminaries. Part 1: Feminism $5.95
John W. Robbins
An analysis of the views of three graduates of Westminster Seminary on the role of women in the church.

The Trinity, Gordon H. Clark $8.95
Apart from the doctrine of Scripture, no teaching of the Bible is more important than the doctrine of God. Clark's defense of the orthodox doctrine of the Trinity is a principal portion of a major new work of Systematic Theology now in progress. There are chapters on the deity of Christ, Augustine, the incomprehensibility of God, Bavinck and Van Til, and the Holy Spirit, among others.

What Do Presbyterians Believe? Gordon H. Clark $6.95
    This classic introduction to Christian doctrine has been republished. It is the best commentary on the Westminster Confession of Faith that has ever been written.

Commentaries on the New Testament

Colossians, Gordon H. Clark	$6.95
Ephesians, Gordon H. Clark	$8.95
First and Second Thessalonians, Gordon H. Clark	$5.95
The Pastoral Epistles (I and II Timothy and Titus)	$9.95
Gordon H. Clark	

    All of Clark's commentaries are expository, not technical, and are written for the Christian layman. His purpose is to explain the text clearly and accurately so that the Word of God will be thoroughly known by every Christian. Revivals of Christianity come only through the spread of God's truth. The sound exposition of the Bible, through preaching and through commentaries on Scripture, is the only method of spreading that truth.

The Trinity Review

    The Foundation's bimonthly newsletter, The Trinity Review, *has been published since 1979 and has carried more than sixty major essays by Gordon H. Clark, J. Gresham Machen, Fyodor Dostoyevsky, Charles Hodge, John Witherspoon, and others. Back issues are available for 40¢ each.*

Order Form

Name _____

Address _____

_____

Please: ☐ add my name to the mailing list for *The Trinity Review*. I understand that there is no charge for the *Review*.

☐ accept my tax deductible contribution of $ ___ for the work of the Foundation.

☐ send me _____ copies of *Three Types of Religious Philosophy*. I enclose as payment $ _____.

☐ send me the Trinity Library of 29 books. I enclose $135 as full payment for it.

☐ send me the following books. I enclose full payment in the amount of $ _____ for them.

_____

_____

_____

_____

_____

_____

_____

Mail to: The Trinity Foundation
Post Office Box 169
Jefferson, MD 21755

Please add $1.00 for postage on orders less than $10. Thank you.
For quantity discounts, please write to the Foundation.